Oh Sweet Om

A CORPORATE JUNKIE'S
SEARCH FOR ENLIGHTENMENT

Om Sweet Om

**A CORPORATE JUNKIE'S
SEARCH FOR ENLIGHTENMENT**

NICOLE LOVALD

ISBN: 978-1-63489-179-0
Library of Congress Catalog Number: 2018959992
Printed in the United States of America
First Printing: 2019
23 22 21 20 19   6 5 4 3 2

Cover design by Jess Morphew
Interior design by Athena Currier

Wise Ink Creative Publishing.
807 Broadway Street NE, Suite 46
Minneapolis, MN 55413
wiseinkpub.com

To order, visit www.itascabooks.com
or call 1-800-901-3480. Reseller discounts available.

Advance Praise

"In a world concerned with what we do, how much we've done, and what we will do next, Nicole asks if we are happy with *who we are*. This shift in focus from a list of accomplishments to evaluating the depth of our authenticity is unnerving yet necessary. While she walks us through her journey from corporate junkie to yogi, she mines readers with questions and suggestions for uncovering your true self. By book's end you can't help but be transformed. You may not feel compelled to leave your day job as Nicole did, but you will better understand what you need to live a life you recognize as your own."

—Kara Douglass Thom, author of *Hot (Sweaty) Mamas: Five Secrets to Life as a Fit Mom*

"A deeply personal memoir, endlessly thought-provoking and enlightening."

—Dan Janal, book coach and author of *Write Your Book in a Flash*

"If you have been sensing for some time that you are on the verge of "a shift," but aren't quite sure what this is or how to go about it, this book is for you! Nicole puts into words the things that are tugging at many of us inwardly. She inspires readers to make little life changes that can lead to surprising and unexpected results . . . Nicole's book is a reminder of how small life changes can take a person in surprising new directions. An inspirational must-read!"

—Heidi Kopacek, psychologist and yoga teacher

"This book serves as a great reminder to us all to cherish life, to relish in the simple things, and to let go of the need to live in a state of constant stress. Nicole opens herself to this change, and I am so thankful to have read this book to allow for opening of myself to the change as well."

—Kristen Trebil-Halbersma, program administrator, child advocate, and yogi

Contents

PART 2: TRANSFORMATION

PART 3: ENLIGHTENMENT

INTRODUCTION

The Journey

"We have taller buildings but shorter tempers . . . more conveniences, yet less time; we have more degrees but less sense; more knowledge but less judgment; more experts, yet more problems . . . more medicine, yet less wellness."

—*Dr. Bob Moorehead*

Growing up, I wanted to be successful. In my mind, "success" looked like a business suit, perfectly highlighted hair, and some trendy—albeit extremely uncomfortable—high heels. I dreamt of living in a big city, having a plethora of successful friends, and exotic vacations I'd brag about to anyone who would listen. Oh, and in this amazing life, I was never, and I mean *never,* going to have kids.

As you can imagine, my definition of success has changed over the years. I've evolved from wanting the picture-perfect *Wall Street Journal* and *InStyle* magazine layouts to what I have now: an inner peace and joy discovered in my search for enlightenment. After years of chasing a dream that wasn't satisfying, I now know that expensive shoes, a six-figure salary, and a high-profile job do not equal an amazing life. I've realized that working long hours, operating on little sleep, and eating terrible meals in front of my computer were never going to lead to unending happiness and fulfillment. On the contrary, I found myself completely stressed out and overwhelmed, both at work and at home.

I was, and still am, married to a military man. Being married to the military brings with it some amazing opportunities and experiences but also a stress that alters your life, for better or for worse. When you are experiencing it, it is hard to see the full impact. Instead, you simply focus on your survival and getting through it. It isn't until you're able to break away from the daily stressors that you begin to realize the intensity of it.

The first deployment we endured as a military family was around the same time I was leaving the nonprofit sector, where I had cut my professional teeth. My husband prepared for his deployment to Kosovo as I prepared to enter the foreign world of corporate life. I had equal parts excitement and apprehension flowing through my veins. I wasn't sure I had what it would take to get ahead in a competitive business environment. I was used to the nurturing aspects of working in social services, but I felt a nagging desire to begin climbing the corporate ladder.

After a few years of settling into cubicle life, deadlines, and never-ending meetings, I found myself changing. I began to recognize a desire to bring something bigger than me into the world. I felt the nudge—or, more accurately, the full-on bodily urge—to have kids.

After becoming a mom, my priorities began to shift (surprise, surprise) and I wasn't willing to put in twelve-hour days, evenings, and weekends to keep moving to the next rung of the ladder. The realization that someone depended on me outside of work opened my eyes to a new way of living.

As I started to evolve into a fully-fledged, diaper-bag-carrying, hand-sanitizer-at-the-ready mom, my husband received his second set of deployment orders. This time, he was headed to war.

His first deployment to Kosovo was for a peacekeeping mission, so I didn't have to spend twenty-four hours a day worrying about him. I knew he was mostly safe (except for that one little uprising event and a few bombings), so I could rest easy at night and continue with my life.

But this one was different. He was scheduled to deploy to Iraq during the height of the war. Everywhere I looked—the newspapers, TV, magazines—it was evident that people were dying where he was headed.

As much as I tried to convince myself that I could handle anything, my mind went into overdrive with dread. I was worried he might be injured. He might be killed. He might come home a different man.

My son would miss his dad and might not even remember who he was when he came home. I kept wondering why we were in this damn war anyway. My mind was in turmoil, and I repeated the same questions to myself over and over. *Why did my husband have to deploy to Iraq? What is going to happen to him? Why do I have to be a single mom and do everything on my own for an entire year?* I know this sounds a bit selfish now, but it was my reality.

On the outside I was keeping it all together, but on the inside I was falling apart. Like most military spouses, I kept a stiff upper lip and attempted to prove to everyone around me that I could handle it. I was determined not to ask for help or to slow down; I would keep up with my work, my parenting, my friendships, my life. I *could* handle it all and *would* handle it all. Until my body told me otherwise.

I began to experience stress in ways I had never experienced before. My hair started to fall out. In clumps. Not just a little hair here and there, but to the point where I was worried I might be going bald. I couldn't eat without getting a stomachache. I would get dizzy anytime I stood up. I was convinced I had some horrible, fatal disease.

Yet I continued to go through the motions day in and day out. I put one foot in front of the other, kept my chin held high, and told everyone I was just fine—great, actually—because I could handle anything.

I'm guessing you've found yourself in a similar position at some point. Your body might have rebelled like mine did, trying to tell you that something needed to change, or you might have noticed a quiet, inner voice asking (or quite possibly begging) you to take notice.

I've met a lot of career-driven people who, in their quest to get ahead, thought they had to do it all. They didn't want to show any weakness, so they continued to pile things on their proverbial plate until something finally broke.

I felt as if my body were ready to break. It hurt too much to physically or emotionally connect to my heart, so I found myself staying busy and working harder to achieve my perfect picture of success. I was suffering physically, mentally, emotionally, and spiritually.

I had an inkling that there was another way. A better way. A way of moving through this stress-filled world with softness and grace. I was craving relief but wasn't quite sure yet where, or how, to find it. But I knew that I had to.

Luckily, I found my way to a yoga mat and was introduced to myself again. The self that had been hidden by layers of stress, striving, and stoicism. The part of me that had been muffled for way too long and was crying to be seen and heard.

My newfound yoga practice began to untangle my life in a very meaningful way. I realized during that time that I was ready to embark on a journey to shift who I was and how I defined success.

Yoga was the conduit to finding my new path. It provided the necessary lessons to teach me how to overcome my striving, worry, and perfectionism. It helped me reconnect to my true self so that I could live a life that was in alignment with what I wanted. It taught me how to manage my stress and how to be more resilient when faced with life's challenges.

My path is my own. Yoga helped me to find my way back to my true self. Your path is your own. I share the story of my journey to yoga to help you find your own way—whether that is through yoga or not doesn't matter. What matters is that you listen to that muffled voice within and start to honor the direction it wants to take you. It will no doubt lead you directly to the same place my yoga practice has led me: the way back home.

PART 1

Awakening

CHAPTER 1

Welcome Home

"You must give up the life you planned in order to have the life that is waiting for you."

—Joseph Campbell

I was miserable during the height of my corporate years, but I couldn't see it. I thought I had everything I had always wanted. I had a decent title, a small staff of people working for me, an office, and enough discretionary money to buy my parents dinner or my friends their drinks at happy hour. I was living the dream.

This dream apparently consisted of feeling overwhelmed and exhausted all the time. I was working myself to the bone, stressed out to the max. I woke up still tired from the day before. I kept thinking there must be something wrong with me, that I must have been sick or worse, because there was no logical explanation for how little energy I had to make it through the day.

As I look back now, I can see that many of my friends were in the same boat, trying to stay afloat while feeling as if they were silently sinking. Many of us are working so hard trying to reach that next destination, the one that we think will fulfill us and lead to euphoria. Instead, we find ourselves feeling completely landlocked and uninspired, dreaming of the next journey. At least, that's how I was feeling.

I can see so clearly now why I was exhausted and con-stantly waiting for someone to throw me a line and pull me to shore. (Forgive me—my dad is a sailor, so I grew up thinking everyone loved metaphors from the sea.)

For over a decade, I woke up at the crack of dawn, wanting nothing but to roll right back over to get a few more hours of sleep. I never felt refreshed when I woke up. Instead, I felt as if I had only shut my eyes for a few minutes until the alarm jerked me away from my precious sleep.

How familiar does this sound? How many days during the week do you wake up only to count the days until the week-end—those two amazing days where you get to roll over and go right back to your precious sleep? (That is, until you have kids. Then you start counting down the years . . .)

When I was finally able to get my overtired self to roll out of bed, I threw on some clothes and running shoes to try to make my way to the treadmill. I wasn't a health nut. I was more concerned about "looking the part," staying thin and perfectly manicured, than I was about my health.

I'm guessing you've been somewhere similar. Or maybe you still are today; forcing yourself up at the crack of dawn so you can get your workout in and fit the mold of the person who has it all together.

I still love to run, but I've learned the importance of balance for my overall health and can honestly say you will never again find me on a treadmill at five in the morning. I've also learned to honor my body and energy; now, if I wake up feeling exhausted, I realize that it's because I need more sleep and less pushing. I need to respect my body and listen to it.

OK, back to the treadmill.

I began my day by waking at that unnaturally early time when the skies are still dark and my neighborhood owl is still quietly singing in the trees. In an effort to get fired up enough to run my mandatory no fewer than three miles a day, I blared my running playlist into my ears.

What kind of music do you listen to at five in the morning to try to get pumped up enough to run three miles? My music of choice was eighties hair bands. Heavy metal. Guns N' Roses. Metallica. Def Leppard. Yep, there is still nothing better in my mind than rocking out with Axl Rose singing "Welcome to the Jungle."

These tunes provided me with the motivation I needed to get through my run, take a shower, and rush out the door for my commute to work. Even though my workout was in part an attempt to do the right thing to be healthy (and to try to look good in my jeans), I now realize it was exacerbating my problems. I started my day in an adrenalized state, which continued as I rushed out the door.

Think about your typical morning for a minute. Do you find yourself in a crazed state, just trying to get out the door to work? That's exactly how I felt each and every day (and this was before I had kids as an excuse!). I went from the treadmill to the shower to rush-hour traffic. On a good day, I might even remember to grab a granola bar so I had a little bit of sustenance on my drive into work.

On my walk from the parking ramp to my desk, I would make a pit stop at the coffee shop. Most days there was a line of fellow corporate junkies looking for their own flavor and fix.

After all this (I'm tired just telling you about it), I would check my daily calendar, only to find that I was in back-to-back meetings from eight to five. My heart would drop and I would begin to feel a tightness in my chest, just thinking about how I was going to feel running from meeting to meeting all day long. I knew that I would be lining my planner with tasks that would eventually need to be accomplished.

I know I'm not alone, that there are a lot of others out there feeling the same way. As I work with life-coaching clients today, I hear similar stories from my fellow recovering corporate junkies and practically anyone with a full-time job.

They share stories of choosing not to drink any liquids so that they don't have to take bathroom breaks. Stories of forgetting to eat all day long and going home absolutely famished and hangry. Stories of putting the kids to bed only to crack open the laptop and put in another four hours of work.

The stories that are the most disheartening to me are the ones of sleeping through the weekend or crashing after the work week so hard that my body breaks down with sickness. I can relate to these stories; I have vivid memories of spending Sunday nights depressed just thinking how this was all going to start all over again on Monday morning.

Do you find yourself experiencing the Sunday night blues?

Do you spend your entire weekend simply recovering from the work week or mentally preparing for the week ahead?

I remember looking around the grey sea of cubicles and seeing the exhaustion in people's eyes. I could feel it on a visceral level, in both myself and those around me. I would walk into work each morning and feel the heaviness in the air. I would smile as I walked past my colleagues and wonder why we were all doing this to ourselves, day in and day out.

One of the final winters I worked in what I so lovingly called "cubicle land," my team and I did a head count each morning to see who was home sick. We celebrated if we had a day when everyone was in the office. The entire team consisted of six people, so this shouldn't have been an Olympian feat, yet somehow it was.

People were dropping like flies from colds, the flu, strep throat, and bronchitis. There were also those unmentioned sick days and medical leaves that we didn't talk about but assumed were the result of mental-health issues (they were finally pushed over the edge!) or stress-induced illnesses.

I experienced all this for years before having kids. It was like the movie *Groundhog Day*, the same story line repeating itself day in and day out.

Once I added a few kids to the equation, I had the perfect cocktail of little sleep, bad food, high stress, and a short temper. I was living on autopilot, stressed out from the moment I woke up to the moment I went to sleep at night. I was trying to do it all, as so many of us are, and was seemingly failing at the most important part.

Do you ever feel like you are failing miserably at everything you do, trying to give yourself 100 percent to your kids or family while also trying to give yourself 100 percent to your work? Do you feel like you are being pulled helplessly in two different directions and don't have the time, energy, or resources to do anything well? That's exactly where I was.

I had an internal drive to succeed at work. I wanted to be successful and reach the pinnacle of my career—to make my parents proud and to prove to myself that I had it in me.

I wanted to provide financially for my family. I wanted to be able to continue to buy rounds at happy hour and dinner for my friends.

What I know now but couldn't see at the time is that my health and well-being are more important than anything else. If I continued to go at the pace I was, something would have to give, and it wouldn't be the work deadlines or demands.

I also didn't realize that who I was was not intrinsically tied to my work persona or what I accomplished. Who I am and what matters most is something found inside of me. It's not something that the rest of the world can see—it's the me that only I can see, hear, and feel. It's the me that can find happiness and contentment without needing a specific title, a certain salary, or any other external validation.

The me that I didn't truly know yet but was on a journey to begin to find.

CHAPTER 2

Stressed-Out

"There is no way to happiness—happiness is the way."

—*Thich Nhat Hanh*

In my striving to do more and always be better, I was causing myself a lot of unnecessary stress. Every decision I made, from which clothes to put on in the morning to what was for dinner that evening, was stressful.

As I looked around me, I knew I wasn't alone in my stressed-out misery. Think about the last conversation you had with your spouse, partner, friends, or family members. How much of the talk revolved around your work stress, your home life stress, your *stress, stress, stress?*

We compare our stories to see who has the most "challenging" life. It's as if we will win a Nobel Prize if we can prove we are suffering more than everyone else at the table. At the time, my conversations at happy hours almost always resulted in little competitions to see who could beat out the others when it came to who had the worst boss, who worked the longest hours or the most weekends. It was as if the person who could prove they had the most miserable workplace won bragging rights and free drinks.

Stress is being called the epidemic of the twenty-first century by experts across the country and even from the World Health Organization[1]. Our generation is more stressed out than any of the generations that came before us. Medical studies have shown that stress is linked to illness, disease, and increased mortality. The American Psychological Association has linked stress to the six leading causes of death[2].

We don't need the experts to give us the stats or prove this to us. We already know. Because we are living it.

We know what stress feels like. We know anxiety and depression firsthand. We know the burning desire to get ahead at any cost.

The cost is our health.

And it's not just us we need to worry about: for the first time in our country's history, children may live shorter lives than their parents[3]. The pressures placed on ourselves and our children are leading to incredible physical and emotional damage.

The rates of anxiety continue to increase in our homes, offices, schools, and playgrounds across the country.

This past Halloween I was in my daughter's kindergarten classroom, celebrating with a small army of princesses and Power Rangers, when there was an announcement for the emergency team to come to the office. My mind immediately went to a food allergy, as there seems to be a peanut allergy in almost every class these days. As much as teachers try to keep the tasty Snickers bars out of their classrooms, I wouldn't be surprised if someone snuck one in. (It was Halloween, after all).

I later found out that an allergic reaction wasn't the culprit. No, it was a child having a panic attack. At an elementary school. During an event that was meant to be fun and playful, not panic-inducing and overwhelming.

What does it say that our children are so stressed out in elementary school that they are having panic attacks? That, during what is supposed to be a fun celebration, they get so worked up that they can't breathe and an ambulance is called?

Whether you realized it before or not, we are surrounded by people feeling anxious or depressed about the pressures of life, the busyness of life, and just life in general. If you are feeling this way, as I was, I hope it provides some comfort to know that you are not alone.

We know we are stressed out. So what? Why does it matter?

Because it is harming our bodies, minds, and spirits. According to the American Psychological Association, stress impacts not only our psychological health but also our musculoskeletal, respiratory, cardiovascular, endocrine, gastrointestinal, reproductive, and nervous systems[4].

Stress impacts everything from our ability to digest food appropriately to our ability to conceive a baby the way nature intended. It also changes the way we breathe, the way our heart beats, how hormones are released throughout our bodies, and the messages our nerves send to our organs, muscles, and brains.

The same research indicated that 77 percent of people regularly experience physical symptoms of stress, such as chronic pain, while 73 percent experience psychological symptoms such as anxiety and depression. Look around you: three out of four people are stressed out to the point that it harms them physically, mentally, and emotionally.

Our bodies are trying to give us messages through the manifestation of physical and emotional pain. If only we would listen to those earlier, more subtle messages. We usually don't listen until we have reached a point where it is no longer optional. We experience panic attacks, depression, autoimmune disease, and dozens of other afflictions that come as a surprise to us.

It shouldn't really come as a surprise, though, as many of us work ourselves to exhaustion Monday through Friday and then find that we crash or get sick on the weekends. We spend our days high on caffeine and then find ourselves coming down midday only to figure out a way (more coffee? chocolate? energy drink?) to push through instead of finding a way to rest and allow our bodies to rejuvenate. The accumulation of our long hours and the demands we place on our bodies and minds during the week reach a head by Saturday, and then we begin to shut down.

The American Institute of Stress cites the top two causes of stress in the US as job pressure and money[5]. In our quest to be successful in our jobs, make more money, and get ahead, our health is falling behind or, quite often, falling apart. That's what happened to me.

My body began to show me signs that I could no longer manage the stress and pressure that it was under. In my quest to hide my worries about my husband being deployed, my desire to be a perfect mom, and drive to succeed at work, I was slowly breaking my body down.

I finally realized I had to do something. I didn't want to continue to feel lousy anymore. I was scared of the constant stomachaches and fatigue. I couldn't figure out why my hair was falling out and I was losing weight (without even trying!). I knew my health and well-being were suffering but felt like I didn't have any control. I wasn't sure what to do or how to do it.

I wanted my doctor to diagnose me with an ailment—an easily treatable one, of course—so she could prescribe a magic pill to make me feel all better. Unfortunately, that didn't happen and I had to continue to search for answers on my own.

On my slow but steady degradation and search for relief, I began reading and learning about how our bodies respond to stress. I learned that when our bodies are under stress, our nervous systems become taxed or heightened and cause biological responses throughout our bodies. I also learned that there is no quick fix or magic pill we can take to calm down our natural stress response and nervous system.

When reading about the nervous system, I was reminded of middle school health class, where we learned about how our bodies respond to stressful situations. At that young age, we couldn't really comprehend what stress was (life was much less stressful for kids when I was growing up), so our teachers provided an analogy our young brains could better understand.

Enter the caveman. That's how the story of stress was first ingrained in my consciousness, all those years ago. My teacher shared that our ancestors didn't have the conveniences that we have and had to hunt for their food and live off the land. In doing so, they were at risk of coming into contact with a mountain lion, tiger, or bear. When they did, their bodies experienced the stress response.

The stress response is activated by our bodies going into high alert and pumping blood to our hearts, focusing on survival. There are then three ways in which we can respond: fighting, fleeing, or freezing. Our bodies respond in one of these ways whether the danger is real or just perceived.

Our bodies are meant to be in this state temporarily, and when we recover from it we are supposed to get back into our "window of tolerance." This is the state where our nervous systems are neither hyper (think anxious) or hypo (think depressed) but are comfortably settled in that happy place that we call homeostasis.

Our natural state—before we came to know stress, seventy-hour work weeks, rush-hour traffic, and unattainable deliverables—is that place where our nervous system is calm, our breath is soft yet steady, and our heart is evenly paced. That relaxed place is accessible to us through meditation, yoga, breath work, and mind-body techniques. Even though we have forgotten what it feels like to be in this natural and beautifully peaceful state, we can relearn how to bring ourselves back to it.

As I was moving through the motions in my corporate life, feeling good about myself and how far I had come, I knew the foundation I had built beneath me was starting to crumble. I was a walking zombie, so tired that there were times I knew I shouldn't be driving for fear of falling asleep on my way home. My energy level would crash every day at about two o'clock and I would have to grab some more caffeine to keep me going. I couldn't keep up with the pace I was trying to live in, and even more distressingly, I didn't feel like there was any way out. (Sound familiar?)

I had confused the notion of success with happiness. I thought that if I worked hard enough, made enough money, and looked the part, I would be blessed with an abundance of joy.

According to former Harvard professor and author of *The Happiness Advantage* Shawn Achor, I had it all wrong[6]. He realized early on in his Harvard career that the students who were most likely to be successful were the ones who had a positive mindset. The students who focused on the good in their lives and experienced gratitude and appreciation for those things—instead of focusing on how hard things were and how hard they had to work— found happiness.

Shawn realized that our society had taught us for generations that happiness revolved around success and that only when we were successful would we find happiness. Thanks to his and others' research in the field of positive psychology, we have learned the opposite is true. If we have an optimistic mindset, we are smarter, more focused, and motivated, and are therefore more successful. As I read his words, I realized I had to not only address my body's messages but also start to focus on my mind. My thoughts and beliefs were impacting my ability to be happy as much as the physical stress I was under. In my quest to reach the pinnacle of "success," I was hurting myself physically, mentally, and emotionally. I needed to learn what Professor Achor's research succinctly taught him: "happiness is the center and success revolves around it." Not the other way around.

Everyone's path to happiness is different. Some people are born with a higher set point for experiencing joy and others need to work to find it. I had been working so hard to do everything right so that I could be successful that I had lost sight of what mattered most.

CHAPTER 3

On My Mat

"Yoga is not about touching your toes. It's about what you learn on the way down."

—Jigar Gor

I'll never forget my first true yoga experience. I had tried some yoga videos and had dabbled in yoga as a form of exercise, but I didn't really understand the capacity of its impact on well-being until a random Friday afternoon. I had recently rejoined the gym to help me shed some post-baby pounds, and the only time I could find to work out was over my lunch hour. As synchronicity would have it, I was drawn to try out a yoga class when I unknowingly needed it most.

I wasn't thinking about yoga as a way to reduce my stress or help me find some semblance of balance. In fact, I wasn't even aware yet that I was out of balance. Tired, yes.

Overwhelmed, yes. But needing to "focus on my health"? No, that was for people who were sick, obese, or suffering from mental illness. My health was just fine. Or so I thought.

As I rolled out my mat on that Friday afternoon and looked around the room, I saw a sampling of your typical corporate gurus talking about meetings, the marathon they were training for, and other BHAG's (big, hairy, audacious goals). I fit right in.

The yoga teacher—people called him Yoga Ted—was a ponytailed hippie with a beautiful smile. He seemed not to have a worry in the world and emitted an almost overwhelming sense of compassion toward the yogis in the room. As he guided us through our poses, he also had us focus on our breathing in a way I had never done before.

As we moved through the postures, my mind began to slowly settle down. If you are like I was during my corporate years, a to-do list perpetually buzzes in the back of your brain, never shutting off. Miraculously, the to-do list faded into the distance, and I could tune into my body without my mind continuously racing.

Have you ever noticed how the mind slows down when you are doing something you love? Psychologists call this being in a state of flow. Athletic coaches sometimes call it "being in the zone."

You experience it when you lose track of time because you are so fully involved in what you are doing. Typically, you are doing something you enjoy so much you fade off into a blissful or concentrated state, and the chatter of your mind becomes quiet. You might become so laser-focused on your task that all other thoughts fade away and the world begins to slow down for you.

That's how I felt in our final pose. Yoga Ted instructed us to lie down on our mats in savasana and relax our bodies and minds. As my eyes closed, I found myself sinking into a beautifully blissful state.

For the first time in as long I as could remember, I didn't think. I didn't move. I didn't do anything. I just lay there and let my breath flow in and out.

I felt a wave of relaxation I had never felt before. I couldn't describe it; I was calm, peaceful, centered, and—dare I say—happy. I wasn't thinking about how many calories I had burned, how I needed to lose just ten more pounds, how I needed to pick up dinner on the way home from work, which sleep method I should be using with my kids, or how I was going to pay all my bills. I experienced a moment of bliss. A moment of homeostasis. A glimpse into what it might feel like to reach enlightenment.

That moment of bliss quickly faded as I rolled up my yoga mat, changed back into my high-heeled shoes, and walked back to my cubicle.

I was left with a feeling that I wanted more of what I had just experienced. I was ready to start to make some changes to make that happen. Other than that yoga class, I wasn't sure where to start, but I knew I desperately needed to begin somewhere.

CHAPTER 4

Slow Change

"Yoga teaches us to cure what need not be endured and to endure what cannot be cured."

—B. K. S. Iyengar

I started to look forward to my Friday yoga class more and more. I began to block out the time on my calendar and schedule my work meetings around it. My best friends could tell if I had been to yoga that week based on my mood. It was slowly but surely starting to change me.

I was learning to slow down and to let my shoulders relax a little bit. I would roll out my mat, lie down, and gently begin to unwind, feeling tension release from my body and mind.

As I moved through the poses, I sunk deeper and reconnected with how it felt to truly be in my body and not just in my mind. I felt my breath steady, and I tuned into my heart beating in my chest. Most importantly, though, my to-do list was off in the distance, out of my mind, and I was finally able to relax.

Off my mat, I began to notice more. I noticed how everyone seemed to have a phone attached to their ear at all times, that they seemed to be in a frenzied state rushing from coffee shop, to meetings, to home.

The next time you are in a restaurant, walking through a mall, or at a concert, look around and see what you notice. It probably won't be a surprise to see how many people are on their phones instead of engaging with the people around them.

How many times have you sat at a table with people you say you want to spend time with, only to check your email or upload pictures onto social media? You might be surprised at how much this occurs when you slow down enough to start to pay attention.

In 2010 the UK government conducted a study on cell phone use and, as a result, created the term "nomophobia" (no mobile phobia)[7]. This phobia refers to anxieties people experience when they are without their mobile devices. The study found that over half of mobile phone users experience anxiety if their battery dies, their phone is lost, or they don't have cell coverage.

Notice how you feel the next time you are without your phone. Do you experience separation anxiety? Does it make you nervous? Are you uncomfortable?

In the US, the statistics outline an even more concerning storyline. Apparently, we are so attached to our phones that we can't keep them out of our bedrooms[8]. Two out of three people sleep with their phones on their bedside table, and a third of cell phone users report to have answered their phones during times of intimacy.

Our addictions to our phones are keeping us from having intimate relationships and real connections. Our "need" to always be attached to our phones keeps us from taking the time to relax and unwind at the end of the day and prepare ourselves for replenishing sleep.

Is this you? Do you feel the need to answer your phone regardless of who you are with or the importance of what you are doing? Think about it for a minute: How often are you ignoring the people you are with to answer a text or check social media? I know I've been guilty of that.

Sometimes our attachment to our phones is by choice, but sometimes it's not. Case in point: I set aside a few hours today to write, for which I need my full attention and limited distractions. I write best in my bedroom, snuggled up in bed, because then I don't see my messy house, the laundry that needs to be done, or the many other things I could be spending my time doing. I also reduce my online distractions by shutting down any social media tabs I might have open and closing out my email. Yet as I typed that last paragraph, my phone dinged five times with different text messages.

Often, after sending us a text message, people expect an immediate response. If they don't get one, they might worry there is something wrong or that we are ignoring them. Maybe you don't care what others think and have no problem not responding; you are obviously much more evolved than I am at this point. I usually choose to respond but let the person (my husband, in this case) know that I am turning my ringer off so I can focus my attention on writing.

How would it feel if you gave yourself permission to take a break from your phone? How would it feel to let go of the attachment to the dinging of your phone, the Facebook likes, and the Instagram feed? Would you feel a sense of freedom? Would it free up time for you to be more fully present with the people in your life?

Many of us crave a sense of community and belonging. We are surrounded by people yet feel completely alone. We have shut ourselves off from our neighbors and live in our own private little worlds, protected by passwords and gated communities. We show fake versions of ourselves on social media so that the world only gets to see what we want them to—the pictures of the perfect life that we have created.

The reality is that many of us are suffering and no one knows. We are going at it alone, waking up and pulling up our bootstraps so that we can take on yet another day. But as we move mindlessly through our waking hours, we know deep down in our souls that something is missing. There has to be more. More connection. More joy. More meaning. More to this one short life that we have been given.

Many of us stay in this state and try to convince our souls that it is enough. Others begin to search. We begin to ask more questions. We begin to seek out connection and meaning. We find others who are in this same state of uncertainty and who are on the path to discovery.

I found those people through yoga. Everyone's journey is their own. My search for another way took me back to my yoga mat. Yours may be an entirely different path. It doesn't matter, as long as you are listening to the universe and honoring the path that is meant for you.

Each time I returned to my mat, it became clearer that the people around me had a commonality. We were a people who were struggling with the same unanswered questions, who were there with the hope of a glimpse of something greater within ourselves. People who were taking a break from the busyness of their world to reconnect with who they truly were, who they had been, or who they might be.

Our yoga mats provide us with the stillness, time, and opportunity to journey into our souls and to uncover what is real for us. How often do you take the time to be still? Do you allow yourself time to quietly venture into your soul and listen to what is trying to be heard? Do you know what is real for you?

Real doesn't always mean comfortable, safe, happy, or perfect. It's the messy us, the us on the inside that we work tirelessly every day to hide from others. It's the us that lives off the cameras, off the social media screens, and out of the corporate boardrooms. The us that is struggling. The us that wants more. The us that knows, deep down, that the journey to the soul is the only place that we can truly connect. Where we can find our true selves, that place inside us where everything is perfect, whole, and complete.

I was beginning to learn and understand that this is our natural state. I realized that, when we are born, we are perfect just as we are. We know no imperfection and haven't been blemished or spoiled by the harshness and realities of the world. We laugh, cry, hug, kiss, and emote freely and unfiltered.

Think about that word for a moment: unfiltered. It means to allow for the purest form; without modifying or refining it in any way. We put structures around our emotions, our thoughts, our love. As we journey from childhood through adolescence and toward adulthood, we learn to contain our feelings and only express that which we believe is accepted by those around us. What would it look like if we allowed our emotions to flow freely without boundaries or limits?

Think about yourself as a young child and the responses you received from the adults in your life when you explored your feelings. Most of us were taught, at a very young age, that we should keep our feelings to ourselves. That they don't belong in the classroom, on the playing field, or even in our own homes. We stuff them. We hold them deep down inside, where no one can see our ugly truth: who we really are. The people who are imperfect because they have thoughts, dreams, and desires that might not match up perfectly with what society supposedly wants for us.

I was learning that our yoga mats give us the place to unlock these emotions and allow us to reconnect with them in a safe and nurturing environment. Yoga mats are where tears can flow, where emotion can be felt, and where healing can occur. On my mat, I could simply sit with my emotions. I could feel them, explore them, and uncover what was inside of me that had been pushed away for years. The exploration felt scary but also safe and healing. It felt like I was being honest with myself for the first time in a really, really long time. It felt like coming home.

CHAPTER 5

The Path

"Do the difficult things while they are easy and do the great things while they are small. A journey of a thousand miles must begin with a single step."

—*Lao Tzu*

The more I experienced on my yoga mat, the more I knew deep down that the corporate world was no longer for me. I knew that the unreasonable deadlines, the stress, my general unhappiness, and the lack of room for creativity were wearing me down. However, the thought of leaving behind all that I had worked so hard for seemed unrealistic and slightly maddening.

It took me years to climb the corporate ladder, and I had finally, *finally*, worked my way up to the title of director. I had earned the title that I believed garnered me respect and a seat at the table where decisions were made. I felt like I had a chance to have an impact.

I was terrified to leave the comfort of a regular paycheck, insurance benefits, and paid vacation. I didn't know if I had what it took to succeed on the "outside." I was scared that I would lose my identity, as I hardly knew myself as anything more than my title, a mom, and a wife. But I knew that to make the transition to a more meaningful, purpose-filled, and joyful life, I had to take the first step and consider some major life changes.

The hardest part was fully accepting that the life that I was living was no longer serving me and meeting all my needs. I had created this life, and I knew that I was responsible for my discontent, so I had to also be responsible for making the necessary changes to live more in alignment with my heart and soul.

The first steps I took were small. I didn't make any major changes overnight. Instead, I began to implement these four steps into my life as it was slowly transforming:

1. Get in touch with your authentic self. Any practice that helps you become quiet so you can reconnect with your inner being will do the job. For me it was yoga; for you it might be meditation, journaling, prayer, or time in nature. Do what works for you.

2. Trust in yourself. We all experience fear, and it's what we do with that fear that matters. If we give into it and allow ourselves to stay stuck, we will never

be open to changing and evolving. Instead, we will limit our opportunities for growth.

3. Take baby steps. You don't have to quit your job, move overseas, leave your spouse, or do anything else drastic to live a more meaningful life. You can start small and dip your toe in the pool without having to dive right in. Transformation doesn't happen overnight. Take your time.

4. Begin making value-driven decisions. What matters most to you? What puts a smile on your face and in your heart? The things you value are important, and when you make decisions that are in alignment with those values, you are allowing yourself to be guided by your intuition.

The business of transformation is not easy. It takes commitment, practice, and a trust in your ability to do hard work.

Glennon Melton-Doyle writes about this in her book *Love Warrior*[9]. She says her family's motto is, "We can do hard things." She recognizes that for transformation to happen, the hard work needs to get done. If we choose the easy way out, we will likely continue to feel stuck, unhappy, like our lives have little meaning. To grow and transform, we become warriors of our own lives and must be prepared to battle our way through to the other side.

During this time of unease and self-discovery, I knew I needed someone to talk to and help guide me, so I found a like-minded therapist. She helped me to understand I was like a butterfly in my evolution. When I first met with her, she said I was in the chrysalis stage, where it's dark and dirty and super uncomfortable.

She explained that, if you can stay with it long enough and do the necessary work, the beauty will eventually evolve and you will transform. While we are fighting our way through the dark parts, we can't always see the light. But if we can hang in there long enough and allow ourselves to grow, shift, transform, we will be amazed by our own evolution.

I knew that to evolve to a place where I could truly embrace the call of my spirit, my intuitive self, the real me, I had to do the work. It took coming to my yoga mat over and over again. It took processing my dreams and desires, uninhibited, with a group of like-minded people. I had to have faith that baring my soul to friends I trusted was not just OK; it was part of the process.

I remember one of these friends telling me a story about how she had a meditation room at home and meditated daily. (She was much more evolved than me. I didn't even have a meditation cushion, let alone a room.) One day, she was irritable and got upset with her daughter, who was quite young at the time. Her daughter said to her, "Momma, do you need your medication time?"

It was an innocent question but at the same time unbelievably wise. As young as she was, she had witnessed and experienced the calming benefits of meditation through her mom. She knew that when all was wrong in Mom's world, she just needed to sit down and get quiet. That is where the beauty happens. That is where transformation begins.

My transformation was slowly happening as I spent more time on my mat and began to explore yoga classes outside of my scheduled Friday afternoon. I started to become more intrigued by the philosophy behind yoga and wanted to know more about the spiritual aspects. I knew that I needed to open myself up to more of this yoga world and that, if I was going to continue to search for enlightenment, I had to go deeper.

CHAPTER 6

Yoga Immersion

"Always do what you are afraid to do."

—Ralph Waldo Emerson

Being the all-in overachiever that I was at the time, I decided that the best way to learn more about this new lifestyle and the changes I was experiencing was to immerse myself in it. Even though I had no desire to be a yoga teacher, I began to search for training programs so that I could learn more about how and why my yoga practice was impacting my life and changing me the way it was. In beautiful synchronicity, I found that a local yoga studio was offering an immersion-based program that started in a little over a month.

At that time, my son was five and my daughter had just turned a year old. My husband had been back from Iraq for a year, but I was still working full-time and was feeling more fatigued and overwhelmed than ever before in my life. Still, I knew I needed to go through with the training now, that I couldn't wait for the "right" time. I knew there was no such thing as perfect timing and figured if I just pushed myself a little bit harder, I wouldn't have a problem making the time for it. I was already used to living my life with more things to get done than my day would allow. How hard could it be to add one more thing in?

Despite the less-than-ideal timing, I convinced myself it could be done and that I needed to make the time for it. I filled out my application so that I could get started the following month.

I had serene visions of completing the training and becoming a completely zen mom, career woman, and wife. I thought that if I studied hard enough, embraced the newfound practices, and became an "official" yogi, I would no longer desire so much change in my life. I thought I would simply learn to love my life as is and be even more grateful for all my many blessings.

Man, was I wrong. Don't get me wrong: it was a transformational experience, and I am a better person for doing it, but not because I became completely zen or learned how to master my downward-facing dog. The physical challenges were certainly a part of it, but it was the mental and emotional challenges that surprised me most. As I look back, I realize that the training made me do the

hard work of reconnecting with myself. My inner self—
the part of me that I had stuffed down, refused to listen
to, and lost touch with long ago.

Whether you find that work through yoga or your own
form of internal exploration, I can tell you it's worth
it in the end. The journey back to your self can be a
profound and eye-opening experience. I had no idea
that what I had signed up for was going to have a last-
ing impact on my life in so many amazing ways. I went
into it thinking that I just needed to learn how to better manage my stress and that, other than that, I had
things figured out.

The reality was that my self-induced stress was kicking my
butt. I thought I needed to learn how to eliminate the
stress from my life (and that yoga was going to show me
how), but I later learned that what I really needed was to
learn how to better manage it.

Stress has gotten a bad reputation in our society, but the
truth is that we need some stress in our lives. It serves
a purpose. It can help us when we need a quick burst
of energy for our protection or productivity. It can help
us when we are competing in a race and need physical
endurance. It can boost our physical and mental abilities
when we need them most.

Stress is meant to be experienced in short bursts. However,
when we live with stress day in and day out, it becomes

problematic. Learning to manage stress is a skill that can be beneficial to anyone, whether you are a yogi or not.

HOW DO YOU LEARN TO MANAGE YOUR STRESS?

1. With awareness: If you don't yet realize the state of your body and mind, you can't begin to make decisions to change it.

2. With your breath: Your breath can be one of your greatest assets when trying to better manage your stress. The most powerful practice you can begin with is to learn how to breathe into your belly. See Part 3 at the end of the book for instructions on how to do this.

3. Keep coming back to this practice, over and over, until you have taught your body a new way of responding.

HOW DO YOU PUT THIS ALL TOGETHER AND REMEMBER IT WHEN YOU NEED IT MOST?

First, you need to recognize the signs that you are beginning to feel stressed-out. Some people might notice a shortness or quickening of their breath, while others might begin to feel a tension headache or uneasiness in their stomach. Everyone experiences stress differently. Begin to pay more attention so that you can find out what your signs are.

Once you notice you are starting to feel stressed-out, simply STOP.

- **S:** Stop what you are doing
- **T:** Take at least three deep, belly breaths
- **O:** Observe the state of your body and mind
- **P:** Proceed mindfully and with intention

This mindful meditation practice can help you become more in tune with what triggers the stress response for you.

When noticing that you are feeling stressed-out, ask yourself the following questions:

- *Is the stress coming from your mind and thoughts?*
- *Is your body tensing up and holding onto the stress?*
- *Does deep breathing help your body begin to calm back down?*
- *How do you want to proceed once you are in a calm state of homeostasis?*

You can use this practice as much as you need to throughout the day until you become aware of the external stimuli causing stress and the internal response you are having to it. After practicing it for some time, you might come to the realization that you do, in fact, have control over the state of your body and mind. Instead of letting stress control your life, you can learn how to manage it for the better.

CHAPTER 7

Sleep Deprivation

"Sleep is the best meditation."

—*Dalai Lama*

As I was sitting through my first weekend of the yoga program, it took everything I had in me just to stay awake. I was exhausted. I had a one-year-old baby at home who wasn't yet sleeping through the night, and my five-year-old was waking up with night terrors.

Every morning I left my house by six o'clock to drop the kids off at daycare and get to work on time. Most days, I was a zombie from sunup to sundown. Our yoga training went from sunrise to ten at night, and I simply didn't have it in me to stay awake and alert while discussing esoteric topics like chakras.

I wanted to show respect to my teachers by actively engaging in the conversations, taking notes, and nodding my head as if I understood what they were saying. In reality, I was only absorbing about half of what they were teaching because my body hurt, my still-nursing breasts were aching for my daughter, and my brain had hit its maximum capacity for the day by about ten in the morning.

As I looked around the room, I felt somewhat isolated in this experience. All my fellow yogis seemed to be well rested and ready for the weekend. They seemed to be actively engaged and enthusiastic and weren't just trying to fake it like I was. Looking around at my teachers and the other aspiring yogis in the group, I felt very alone.

But looking at our society as a whole, I knew that I wasn't alone. According to the American Psychological Association, stress keeps 40 percent of adults lying awake at night[10]. With minds racing, nearly half of adults stare at their ceiling or desperately attempt to count sheep so that they can wake up feeling refreshed.

Our relationship to stress is impacting our ability to have undisturbed sleep. Our constant worrying and the ruminating thoughts that flow through our minds make it difficult, if not impossible, to get a good night's sleep. As a culture, we are a very tired group of people.

Think about it for a minute: When was the last time you had a full night's sleep without waking up to go to the bathroom, checking your phone, or looking at the clock?

You might be one of the lucky ones who can sleep through the night. But do you wake up feeling well rested? Even if we do sleep our eight hours, many of us wake up feeling like we need more. We wake up feeling groggy and irritable instead of energized and ready to take on the day the way our bodies are designed to.

We learn at a young age not to value sleep (neither the amount nor the quality). Our busy schedules of after-school activities, sports, and homework keep many children from getting the amount of sleep their bodies need. When we get to college, we pull all-nighters before finals and live by the motto, "I'll sleep when I'm dead."

As adults, we engage in break-room battles to see who can claim the least amount of sleep and receive the highest honor of respect from our leaders, our colleagues, and our employees. But the wounds are real, and our health is suffering because of it. Sleep deprivation, stress, and adrenal fatigue are the hallmark ailments of the twenty-first century. We are working our bodies to complete exhaustion and are not taking the necessary steps to replenish ourselves.

In my search of enlightenment and improved health and wellness, I was completely burnt out. My fellow yoga trainees (we called ourselves the sangha sisters) all seemed to have already embraced what I was just beginning to learn. They already knew the importance of self-care and seemed to be incorporating it into their lives.

As I listened to their stories about stopping on their drive to our weekend together to get a massage (OK, this could have just been one or two, but in my mind they all got massages), I assumed they had something I didn't. I assumed they had more time or resources than I did.

In reality, what they had was an understanding that if they didn't take care of themselves, they wouldn't have the energy they needed for the sitting and learning that we were going to do all weekend. They had learned that self-care wasn't selfish and wasn't something to be neglected. They understood it wasn't a luxury but a necessity.

I often ask my coaching clients what their self-care practices are. More than once I've had clients ask me, "What is self-care?" I thought they were joking at first, but realized by their blank stares that they were dead serious.

James Gordon, the director of the Center for Mind-Body Medicine, declares that "self-care is healthcare"[11]. In other words, our care of self is what keeps us in a state of health.

I used to think that self-care was a luxury—an annual massage or the rare mani-pedi. What I've come to understand is that it is so much more. Self-care encompasses all the things you do to take care of yourself. It includes the things you enjoy and that fill you up, such as reading a book, going for a walk outside, or going to a movie alone. It can include eating nourishing and healthy foods (because you know you feel better when you do). Your self-care might include taking a few moments to check in with your breath, quietly meditate, or think of the things in your life you are grateful for.

Self-care practices are what help to keep you in balance so that you can move through your days with more energy and ease. They are practices that you incorporate seamlessly into your life so they don't become one more thing that you *have* to do but instead something that you *get* to do and look forward to.

Do you have any enjoyable daily practices that inadvertently help to take care of you? If not, let me suggest some for you to try out. Don't worry, I'm not asking you to add more into your day; I'm asking you instead to use your time more wisely, doing the things you enjoy.

SELF-CARE PRACTICES:

FOREST BATHING (otherwise known as simply getting outside) has been proven to reduce the stress hormone cortisol and help your immune system[12]. Bring your dog for even more of a boost in anti-stress hormones.

TAKE A HIKE. Literally. Get in some green space and move your body. Leave your phone at home for even more benefit.

BREATHE. Take a few deep breaths and relax your body and mind.

MEDITATE. Bring your awareness to the present moment. What do you see? Hear? Feel? Close your eyes and meditate or light a candle and gently gaze at the flame. Whether it's one minute or ten doesn't necessarily matter. Just taking a break to slow down and let go of distractions can reduce your stress and help you calm down.

GIVE YOURSELF A HUG. I know it sounds corny, but your body doesn't know the difference between an embrace that comes from someone else and one from your own hands. Neuroscience has found that crossing your arms over the midline of your body tricks the brain and helps to reduce pain[13].

FIND WHAT WORKS FOR YOU. Maybe it's reading a magazine or book. Maybe it's singing in the shower. What calms you down might sound like a traumatizing experience to others. It doesn't have to be something incredibly time consuming or expensive. Your self-care practice should be something you enjoy that you can add into your day without tremendous effort.

Add one thing to your day and see what slowly begins to unfold. You might be surprised at how, over time, something so small, like giving yourself a hug, can have a major effect on your life.

CHAPTER 8
A Yogi's Self-Care

"Change is not something that we should fear. Rather, it is something that we should welcome. For without change, nothing in this world would ever grow or blossom, and no one in this world would ever move forward to become the person they're meant to be."

—B.K.S. Iyengar

As I sat with my legs crossed, Mexican blanket underneath my sits bones (I had never before paid attention to the bones I sit on, nor did I know they had a name), I listened to our teachers talk about self-care. Their self-care philosophy came from the traditional yogi's practice, Ayurveda.

Ayurveda philosophy is more all-encompassing than the Western system of health we are used to. Ayurveda looks at the whole self—body, mind, and spirit—to figure out where imbalances have occurred and then uses nutrition, self-care, and movement to come back to a state of balance.

During this session, we learned about daily self-care practices called sadhana. With my eyes burning and bloodshot, I sat and listened as we were guided through what our daily ritual should be (if we were to be real, card-carrying yogis).

We were advised that, upon waking, we should get out of bed and do an hour-long asana or physical yoga practice. That would open our bodies for the twenty-minute meditation we were then to complete. Following meditation, we should give ourselves a full-body oil massage (abhyanga). Then we could shower, scrape our tongues, brush our teeth, and dress for the day.

The morning routine continued with meal preparation. We were to make all our meals for the day that morning, from fresh, organic ingredients. We were told we shouldn't be eating leftovers or food that wasn't just cooked, as it won't hold onto its life force and will therefore lose most of its nutritional value.

I stared at these women in total disbelief and asked myself what the hell I had gotten myself into. I looked around at my sangha sisters to see if they had the same looks of horror on their faces.

Much to my surprise, however, they didn't. They were taking copious notes and asking questions like: How much oil do I use? Where do I buy a tongue scraper? What kind of yoga do you recommend in the morning?

Say what? I hit snooze on my alarm three times before I finally rolled out of bed, took a three-minute shower, fed my kids, poured some coffee down my throat, and maybe remembered to grab a granola bar on my way to work. Did I mention these women didn't drink coffee either? Just green tea. Straight up.

I realized in that moment I was not among "my people" anymore. I was used to being around people who were completely stressed out all the time, complaining about how much they had to do and how little time they had to do it in. The women around me seemed much more relaxed and at ease with their lives.

This was infuriating. They obviously didn't have to struggle through the fast-paced life that I had created for myself. At the same time, it was an incredibly liberating moment for me. They proved to me that there was another way.

The realization that there was a way out—not just for me but also for my friends, family, and colleagues—was groundbreaking for me. I quietly promised myself that I was up to the task. I wasn't necessarily looking forward to a two-hour morning routine, but I was ready to find some space in my life. I was ready to allow myself to be more open and to learn from the women around me. I was ready to do the hard work.

CHAPTER 9

Redefining Success

"The success of Yoga does not lie in our ability to perform postures but in how it positively changes the way we live our life and our relationships."

—*T. K. V. Desikachar*

When I returned home from a weekend immersion with my sangha sisters, I felt completely reenergized. My husband was spending my weekends away having quality time with the kids. It was a great opportunity for him to get a taste of my experience as a single parent while he was gone. That's not to say that he wasn't under an immense amount of pressure and who knows what else while he was deployed, but it's certainly not easy parenting on your own either.

No one warns you how hard it is to be a parent. They certainly share the highlights with you and tell you that "your life will change in so many unimaginable and amazing ways." What they don't tell you is how tired you will be. They don't share how overwhelming it is to manage a job, a marriage, and the full-time needs of children.

It is a beautiful experience, no doubt. But it's also hard. It was a nice break for me to get away for my teacher training every few months. The change of scenery alone felt as if it were good for my soul.

Following the first weekend away, my husband commented on how bright and vibrant I looked. I felt it too. I could stay alert later at night, I was inspired to study, and I just felt more content overall. It would last for a few days, but then the busyness and lack of sleep would take their toll again and I would go back to feeling overwhelmed, uninspired, and just generally lousy. I wanted to immerse myself more into this new yoga world but was terrified to leave the safety of the full-time working world.

The next time we met for our training, I talked with one of my sisters about how challenging it was for me to find the time to do all the studying, sadhana practices, and work involved with the training. I shared that I would love to quit my job so that I could do more training, but that then I wouldn't have the money I would need to do it.

Through that conversation, we came to the conclusion that you can have time or money, but you can't have both. She was a full-time stay-at-home mom. She had all kinds of time (granted, I wouldn't call it *free* time), but she didn't have the finances to do all the trainings she wanted to. I had the money but didn't have the time to truly do the work I knew was needed. We wondered as we talked, "Is there any way to have them both?"

This isn't the point in the book where I share some amazing scheme that will bring the dollars rolling in while you travel the world learning more about yoga and chillaxing. But it is where I mention trust in the universe and the belief that we can manifest abundance.

In Gabby Bernstein's book, *The Universe Has Your Back,* she writes about having faith in the journey we are on and that the more open we are and the more we ask for what we want from the universe, the more often we will get it[14]. If we assume we won't have the time or the money, we shouldn't be surprised when we feel strapped by both.

If instead we focus our energies on what it is that we do want in our lives, we may begin to see some answers to our prayers slowly unfold.

It's a simple cause-and-effect exercise. We can explore why things happen and the results that come from them all day long, but the bottom line is that our thoughts, beliefs, and behaviors create our reality.

You can look at it through the philosophical concept of the law of attraction, which is the belief that focusing your thoughts in a positive or negative way will manifest in either positive or negative experiences in your life. People who believe in the law of attraction think that by professing what you want and having faith, it will come to fruition.

Have you ever seen this happen in your life? Have you spent time focusing on what you want to bring into your life or change and then, suddenly, it began to happen? Welcome to the law of attraction. Our thought patterns create our energy, and our energy attracts what it is that we are thinking about and manifesting (or wanting).

It's best explained with the famous saying often attributed to Gandhi:

> *"Your beliefs become your thoughts,*
> *Your thoughts become your words,*
> *Your words become your actions,*
> *Your actions become your habits,*
> *Your habits become your values,*
> *Your values become your destiny."*

I was beginning to redefine the way I was looking at things. My success was no longer intrinsically related to how much I was accomplishing but was beginning to be more about how I felt and whether I was living in harmony with my beliefs and values. I was slowly shifting my thoughts from what was lacking and keeping me from having success to embracing all the good in my life and feeling gratitude and appreciation for those things.

As my mindset was shifting, so was my reality. The universe was beginning to open in ways that were new to me, and my life was slowly changing. I was finding more ease in my day-to-day and, as a result, could let go of my grip on what I expected and allow more flow to come in. In doing so, I was feeling more and more stress melt away and was becoming more resilient to my daily challenges.

As I was becoming clearer about what it was that I wanted in my life—more time, space, ease, and joy—I was beginning to experience what that felt like. My definition of success was no longer having the money to buy all the material things I wanted or the prestige that came along with it. I wanted simplicity. I wanted more time, with my kids, my friends, and myself.

As my definition of success changed and my mindset shifted to support these new values, the universe was beginning to have my back.

CHAPTER 10

Living Yoga

"I have been a seeker and I still am, but I stopped asking the books and the stars. I started listening to the teaching of my soul."

—*Rumi*

The next time I attended my training weekend away, we were given a bunch of homework. To me, yoga homework was a very scary idea.

I'm used to relying on my left brain, especially for work that involves processing thoughts, ideas, philosophies, and experiences. I wasn't used to homework that involved using my body, turning inward to my soulful thoughts and feelings, or noticing how my energetic body responded to the practices. It was time to tap into my right brain, home of my dormant creative and expressive side.

The homework that we were tasked with involved doing yoga. Doing *a lot* of yoga.

We were required to attend several classes so that we could critique the teachers and look for what we liked, what we didn't like, and what we swore we would never, ever do. It's interesting how, when you think of yourself as the expert in the room, you can suddenly find all kinds of things you'd never do or say.

The other piece of the homework was to begin to develop a home practice. Our teachers explained that a home practice was a way to integrate yoga into your daily lives.

As you can imagine, I immediately panicked when the teachers started to talk about our assignments. I timidly raised my hand and said, "I'm sorry, but I just don't know how I can possibly complete all this homework while working full-time and with two small kids at home. Is there any other way I can complete the requirements?"

My teachers were reasonable people and genuinely wanted to see us all succeed. They assured me I could handle it and began to explain to the class what "Living Your Yoga," the name of our program and the philosophy on which it was based, meant. I didn't fully understand it, just as I hadn't fully understood the nature of yoga, until they provided their definition.

They explained that most of us think of yoga as a physical practice where you move your body from position (asana) to position and sometimes end up looking like a human

Gumby. However, that was a small and somewhat minor component of the overall yoga philosophy and practice.

Yoga is a Sanskrit word that means "union" or "to yoke." *Yoga* is to come together as one, to make yourself whole again, to reunite with your true self. Living your yoga is committing to the practices and living in a way that brings you back to your center. It's bringing you home to the union of body, mind, and spirit.

Hearing their definition, I began to reflect on my pre-yoga life and what I was like in the corporate world. I realized that I had not been living in a way that was connected to my body, mind, and spirit. I was spending my days, from the moment I woke up to when I went to bed, in my head listening to my thoughts on repeat. It was a rare occasion when I noticed any sensation or feeling in my body, and it was only on my yoga mat that I felt like I was connected to my spirit.

I know I wasn't alone in this either. You don't need to commit to a yoga teacher training program, or even yoga for that matter, to recognize that you are living in a disconnected way. Some of us live our lives constantly in our heads.

Researchers have estimated that we have anywhere from fifty thousand to seventy thousand thoughts per day. Of those thoughts, approximately 90 percent of them are repeats and 70 percent of them are negative in nature[15]. We think about what we have done wrong, what we should be doing, and all the ways in which we aren't living up to our own standards and expectations.

In life coaching, we refer to these thoughts as our "inner gremlins," a term coined by psychotherapist and author Rick Carson[16]. He shares that our minds are the main cause of our suffering and that, if we can learn to quiet our thoughts, we can find some respite from the miserable stories we've created in our heads.

Take a few minutes and just sit and listen to your thoughts. What do you notice? Are your thoughts kind? Are they supportive? Are they true? Are they necessary? Often, they are none of these things.

Many of our thoughts are accusatory in nature or, at the very least, unkind. We talk to ourselves in condescending and hurtful ways. If you listen closely, you may find that you would never, ever speak to anyone else in the way that you talk to yourself.

Here is your personal invitation to begin to change your thoughts.

You read that right—you can change your thought patterns. As much as we've been taught to believe that our minds make us who we are, that's not true. The real us is the inner self, the self I was learning to connect to. The self on the inside that feels and doesn't just think. The self that knows what is best for us.

Let's take a few moments to go back to watching your thoughts. This time, imagine you are lying in a field on the bright green grass, looking up at the vibrant blue sky. As you lie on your back, watch the clouds slowly drift by and out of sight.

Now, imagine your thoughts are like the clouds. Your whole self—mind, body, and spirit—is vast like the blue sky. The clouds are simply visitors, drifting in and out of your awareness.

Notice the qualities of the clouds. Are they big or small? Can you see where they come from? Do they look dark and scary or beautiful and light? What else do you notice about them?

Now, as you notice your thoughts drift across your awareness, ask yourself the same questions. With the same kind of curiosity you had for the clouds, be curious about the nature of your thoughts. Then, just as you watched the clouds slowly float away and out of your sight, allow yourself to let go of your thoughts.

Easier said than done, I know. With repetition, it will become more and more natural to notice your thoughts and then let them go. Our attachment to our thoughts brings us a lot of pain and suffering. Learning to let go of our thoughts and to realize they don't define us can bring a sense of freedom.

All of this helped me understand why I felt so good after my yoga classes. It was the only time I was slowing down enough to quiet my mind and feel what it was like not to have those fifty thousand thoughts whirling through my head. It allowed for a space to be created so that I could feel centered and experience my whole being. I was getting out of my headspace. I wasn't trying to analyze anything. I was allowing myself to simply be. To experience what it was like to reconnect with my whole self.

What I was hearing from my instructors was that by "living my yoga," I could take these practices off my mat and begin to be more connected and in union with my whole self throughout my days. They were telling me that I didn't need to wait for a certain time or place to connect with myself; I could eventually learn how to be in that state all (or at least most) of the time.

They went on to explain that yoga uses a philosophy of eight limbs to reach "samadhi," or enlightenment, that beautiful state of being in union. I was intrigued by this philosophy and wanted to learn more. I had become familiar with the eight Buddhist precepts from my own self-study but had not yet learned about the eight limbs of yoga. If this was going to be my how-to guide to enlightenment, I was all in.

CHAPTER 11

The Eight Limbs of Yoga

"Change is not something that we should fear. Rather, it is something that we should welcome. For without change, nothing in this world would ever grow or blossom, and no one in this world would ever move forward to become the person they're meant to be."

—B. K. S. Iyengar

Originally handed down orally, the eightfold path, or eight limbs, were documented by a man named Patañjali in a book called the *Yoga Sutras*[17]. The *Yoga Sutras* outlines the nature of our mind; how to connect the mind, body, and spirit; and ultimately how to reunite with our inner consciousness. The path, when practiced fully through yoga, can lead to less suffering, less ego, less attachment, and a greater sense of wholeness and connectedness with our divine or inner selves.

When most people think about yoga, they think about it as exercise with stretching. Most people don't realize that there is so much more to yoga than the physical practice. We are used to seeing intricate and beautiful poses on the cover of the *Yoga Journal,* all over our Instagram feed, and in our gyms.

As we began to cover more about the eight limbs in my class, I was surprised to learn that they don't begin with the physical practice that we have become so accustomed to thinking of when we hear the word yoga. The physical aspect is just one limb—Asana. The rest concern our internal and external disciplines that provide a foundation for moral conduct. Having grown up in a Lutheran household, I would liken these to the Ten Commandments but without all the authoritative dogma attached.

Two of the limbs, Yamas and Niyamas, are guidelines that provide the dos and don'ts of being a yogi. Some might say you can't be a yogi without complete adherence to these, but most believe instead that they give you something to work toward, to focus on, and to provide direction on your path.

Keep in mind that you don't need to have the desire to be a yoga practitioner to apply some of the wisdom of these tools to your life. If you are a stressed-out corporate junkie like I was, they can help provide a foundation for overall wellness.

The yamas are tools or moral considerations that can ultimately help you to lessen your suffering. If you can learn how to embody these five practices, you will likely experience a lot less heartache (self-induced and otherwise) throughout your life. They provide the keys to living a life with more freedom and, quite possibly, joy.

They break down into ahimsa (nonviolence), satya (truthfulness), asteya (not stealing), brahmacharya (behavior moderation), and aparigraha (non-greediness). These all seemed to be ethical considerations that I could get behind. I knew I wasn't adhering to them 100 percent of the time, but they were certainly things I was willing and able to work on.

In addition, I learned that Patañjali didn't believe we were sinful beings if we didn't adhere to these; instead, he believed in cause and effect—that, naturally, we would cause ourselves unnecessary suffering if we didn't commit to these disciplines. This was a nice reprieve from the religious beliefs that I grew up in, which taught we were all inherently sinful regardless of the choices we made or how we lived our lives.

You might be wondering how these can apply to your life. In other words: How can you relate to these ethical practices?

Think about your daily life for a moment.

AHIMSA

How often are you doing or saying things to yourself that are violent? Being unhealthy is being violent to yourself. Do you tend to self-medicate with food, alcohol, or drugs? How often does your inner dialogue tell you that you are stupid, fat, ugly, or uncreative?

SATYA

How often do you bite your tongue and not say what you are really thinking? Are you being true or honest with yourself throughout your days? Are you willing to have the hard conversations that need to happen or do you continue to shy away from confrontation?

ASTEYA

Do you ever take credit for other people's work or in a subtle way not give others credit for the work they've done? Have you ever taken something that doesn't belong to you? Do you steal conversations away so that you can be the center of attention?

BRAHMACHARYA

Do you live in a balanced and moderate way? Have you found yourself filling all the hours of your day, trying to always have more fun, adventure, success, friends, intelligence, or experience?

APARIGRAHA

Do you give in to greed and always want more material things, like a bigger house, better car, and money? Do you feel entitled to have certain things in your life and believe that you deserve to have more than others? Have you found yourself constantly striving to do more, have more, be more?

These are all examples of how our lives can be out of balance. Learning how to live with greater moderation, having more acceptance and appreciation for what you do have, speaking your truth with honesty and integrity, and living from a place of compassion can help you experience moments of enlightenment (even if you aren't a yogi).

We then learned that the niyamas are internal disciplines or behaviors that only you know about and are responsible to yourself for. They aren't necessarily behaviors that you put out into the world but practices and philosophies that you internalize to assist with your overall growth and continued transformation.

Similar to the yamas, they can be used as guideposts for making decisions about how you live your life. The niyamas are sauca (purification), santosha (contentment), tapas (discipline), svadhyaya (self-study), and ishvara-pranidhana (dedication to the divine).

As I learned more about the niyamas, I could hear Yoga Ted and my other yoga teachers' words reflected in them. I had been learning about the importance of these practices without realizing it. My teachers had talked about living healthfully (sauca) and being content with who and where we are in our life (santosha). They had also talked about the importance of committing to our practice and using curiosity to explore our beliefs, bodies, and minds (svadhyaya). I had also heard many teachers talk about our inner self, spirit, soul, deities, and source. Without specifically naming it or labeling it, they were teaching dedication to the divine (ishvara-pranidhana).

Again, you might be wondering how these apply to you. Let's take a moment and see if the following questions can help you connect to these concepts in a meaningful way.

SAUCA

What are some of the things you can do to have a healthier body and mind? Do you take breaks from your computer throughout the day to move your body and stretch? Can you stop eating lunch at your desk or skipping meals altogether? How about a quick meditation break to find your center when things get crazy?

SANTOSHA

Do you take time to feel grateful for all the good things in your life? Can you look around your home or at your relationships and find people or things that bring you a sense of deep contentedness? Can you let go of all your striving and enjoy simply being?

TAPAS

Where in your life would more discipline be beneficial? Have you been trying to implement an exercise routine but need to commit? What would it take for you to cultivate some new habits to support your goals? (Not sure? Don't worry, we will address this more later.)

SVADHYAYA

Do you ever take the time to pause and contemplate why you responded in a certain way to a challenging situation? Can you uncover how and why you react to people or situations that push your buttons? Have you ever asked yourself, "Why do I do that? Where does that come from? How could I adjust/change/adapt?"

ISHVARA-PRANIDHANA

What are your personal spiritual practices? What brings you closer to your true self? Can you articulate your spiritual or religious beliefs in a way that feels true and meaningful to you? Do you take time to connect with those beliefs or practices?

Hopefully some of these questions helped you see a connection to how the niyamas can apply to your life. As I learned more, they seemed to resonate on a personal level for me.

In fact, I had been searching for a spiritual philosophy since having some disagreements with the Lutheran church that grew up in. I wanted to have a foundation on which to teach my kids right from wrong and how to treat yourself and others. I had struggled to find a philosophy that felt right for me. I finally felt as if I had found my answer.

After learning more about the yamas and niyamas, we began to dig into the third limb, Pranayama—breathwork. At first, I couldn't understand why we need to have an entire limb or practice devoted to breathing when we breathe naturally all day, every day. It wasn't until later that I learned the utmost importance of how we breathe and the incredible impact it can have on our overall well-being.

The next time you are startled, nervous, or upset, notice how you are breathing. Take note of how your breath changes when you are feeling sad or depressed. Typically, when we are stressed out or anxious, we tend to take short and jagged breaths into our chests. When we are depressed or lethargic, we take long and sometimes irregular breaths.

Our breath can mirror our emotions. By watching our breath and being curious about it, we can begin to understand more about our emotional states. Not only can our breath be an indicator that we are experiencing a challenging emotion, but it can also be the tool that we use to bring ourselves back into a state of balance.

We can control our breathing and even manipulate it in a way that can be energizing to our bodies, calming to our minds, and relaxing to our bodies. Our breath, called "prana" in Sanskrit, is our life force. When we have no breath, we have no life. It brings with it healing, universal energy and necessary oxygen to keep us functioning healthfully.

HOW CAN WE USE OUR BREATH TO LEARN MORE ABOUT OUR EMOTIONAL STATE?

Here comes that meditation again: STOP. You read that correctly; put the book down and stop for a moment (OK, read the rest of the instructions first so you know what to do when you put the book down).

S—Stop what you are doing

T—Take a few breaths

O—Observe your breath and body

- Are you breathing into your chest?
- Are you breathing into your belly?
- Are your breaths long or short?
- Jagged or smooth?
- How does your body feel?
- Do you feel tension anywhere in your body?

P—Proceed with your previous activities with greater awareness, or take a few moments to use the breath work in the Part 3 to bring your body into a greater state of balance.

After learning all about how our breathing patterns are an integral part of our yoga practice, we moved on to the final limbs.

I was surprised to learn that three of the limbs focused completely on inner awareness. Our ability to connect inwardly was necessary before we could reach enlightenment. I was so used to focusing my energy on my outer world that this really threw me.

What my teachers were telling me was that to reach the final limb, enlightenment (Samadhi), I had to learn to turn inward, withdrawing my senses from the outer world (Pratyahara). I then had to learn to focus or concentrate completely on my inner self (Dharana) and finally master the art of meditation (Dhyana). All this time I thought yoga was about moving and breathing, not stillness. This threw me for a loop.

Experiencing stillness was incredibly hard for me. How could I be still when I had a husband and two little kids at home, worked full-time, and needed to somehow manage all the responsibilities that came with those? Now I had three limbs to work on to learn how to embrace stillness.

What struck me most throughout this conversation, though, was how I could begin to find meaningful ways to integrate all this into my already busy life.

My teachers shared that even if I just got down onto the floor and played with my kids mindfully, that could be my daily practice. If I started to take a few more deliberate breaths throughout the day or found three minutes to meditate, that was my yoga. They assured me that I didn't have to master all the limbs overnight. It would take time before they became second nature and an integrated part of my life.

I was feeling a lot more optimistic after that talk and was determined to figure out a way to do my homework, even if it meant I could only commit to the practice a few minutes each day.

Every day I tried to find a way to do some yoga. Whether it was taking a child's pose in my living room while my kids climbed all over me or finding a few quiet minutes to meditate, I was determined to do my homework.

Slowly but surely, it was becoming a part of my life. I was starting to integrate the practices when and where I needed it most. One day, I was soothing my baby in the ER after she spent the whole night screaming with an ear infection. As I sat in the treatment room waiting for the doctor to come in, she finally fell asleep.

As I held her in my arms, I quietly turned inward (for probably the first time in over twenty-four hours) and realized how tired, overwhelmed, and just plain cranky I was. Rightfully so. But in that moment I realized the thing that would serve me most and help me calm and take care of myself was to meditate.

As I let my overwhelmed brain quiet down, I began to match the breathing of the sweet baby in my arms. I felt my body begin to soften and relax. In the few minutes I had before the doctor came in, I had found a way to hit the reset button.

After the realization in the ER that I didn't need the "perfect" time to practice, I started to find more ways to add my yoga into my life. I did restorative yoga in my daughter's bedroom after putting her in her crib (because all hell would break loose if she didn't know I was still in her room ready to soothe her). I found myself taking deeper and fuller breaths in the bathtub or shower.

I was slowly beginning to live my yoga. It was becoming a way of life for me. I was still busy and still overwhelmed a lot of the time, but I was noticing how I felt more often (in both my body and mind) and was using what I had learned to calm myself and turn inward, even if for only a few moments.

Don't get me wrong—I was still tired. I was still dreading my cubicle life. But I was also surrendering to all of it differently. In this new way, I was learning how to accept my life and even appreciate some of the more challenging times.

It also started to wake me up even more to how much the corporate world no longer fit for me. How instead of talking to my employees about their service-level agreements I wanted to talk to them about their goals, dreams, and desires. I no longer wanted to go to happy hours where we gossiped about our colleagues, drank too much, and regretted it in the morning. I wanted to continue to uncover my layers, to be completely and unabashedly authentic, with no apologies or regrets.

As you begin to implement some or all of these practices, you will undoubtedly begin to question certain aspects of your life as well. Don't worry—you probably don't need to quit your job tonight or run off and become a yoga teacher (although, if you do, that's OK too!).

Instead, try the steps below:

1. Sit with the questions that come up for you.

2. Acknowledge them and become curious about them.

3. Adopt a "beginner's mind" and question how and why you feel the way you do.

4. Ask for guidance from your inner self, Spirit, God, the universe, or whatever higher power you resonate with.

5. Continue this practice until you feel you have the clarity you desire.

Be forewarned: when you start to change, people may or may not begin to see the new you and accept you as you are.

I began to make new friends and slowly distance myself from some of my older friends. I gravitated toward like-minded people, and they gravitated toward me. I found myself slowly building a community of souls who I liked to call "seekers." People who weren't comfortable with the status quo. People who couldn't sit still, doing the same thing day after day, when their soul spoke to them and urged them to move. You might start to notice the same change in your life.

I found that living my yoga was changing my life—from my friendships, to my work satisfaction, to how I was raising my kids. It was becoming a part of me and I it. A beautiful yet subtle transition was happening as I was transforming from the inside out. I was not only living my yoga; I was becoming my yoga.

CHAPTER 12

The Meltdown

"I will not die an unlived life. I will not live in fear of falling or catching fire. I choose to inhabit my days, to allow my living to open me, to make me less afraid, more accessible, to loosen my heart until it becomes a wing, a torch, a promise. I choose to risk my significance, to live so that which came to me as seed goes to the next as blossom, and that which came to me as blossom, goes on as fruit."

—*Dawna Markova*

When doing the work of reconnecting with yourself, there will inevitably be great ups and downs. This is the undeniable and inescapable rollercoaster of life. Just when things seem to be going perfectly and everything makes sense, your world will turn upside down.

This happened to me during our third immersion session. That weekend, we were to teach in front of others for the first time. We had to take what we had learned and show our instructors and peers that we had the practices not only in our minds but also in all levels of our bodies and souls.

When it was time to teach my class, I asked my inner self for guidance and support. As I taught the class, I felt as if it weren't really me teaching it. Instead of hearing my voice crack and feeling my hands tremble and face turn red, as was the norm for my corporate presentations, I felt calm and in control. As I rested my hands at my heart and bowed my head with my final namaste, I knew that yoga was now an integral part of my life. It was in me. It was a part of me.

I've always hated the part of the rollercoaster ride when you are slowly going up, up, up and hear the rattling of the chains, knowing that at any moment you were going to begin to drop and feel the pit in your stomach. After teaching my class that day and taking a break, we felt our high plummet to a new low.

Our teachers said that they were disappointed in the classes that we had just taught. They felt as if we hadn't fully embodied the teachings quite yet. Looking around the room at my sangha sisters, I could see the devastation in their faces and feel the heaviness of what was just shared. We felt as if we had failed. We had shared ourselves in a very vulnerable way and were told that we hadn't met our teacher's expectations.

We've all felt that sense of failure before and know how uncomfortable it can be. Maybe you disappointed a spouse or boss. Maybe you felt it growing up, when your parents were upset with you.

After learning that we had let our teachers down, I didn't want to feel the pain and sense of failure that it brought up for me. I was exhausted, overwhelmed, and terrified I had done the wrong thing by signing up for this training.

I wanted the safety of what was known and comfortable, so I called my husband for comfort. I cried to him and told him I was sure I wasn't going to graduate and that I had failed my teachers. I was a failure and was stupid for thinking this was a good idea. I apologized, through tears, for choosing to do this course that took me away from him and our kids, who I loved and wanted to be with more than anything in that moment. I just wanted to go home. I wanted to hide. I wanted my life to return to what it was before I started doing all this internal work.

I was humiliated but knew it would be even more humiliating to leave at this point. I couldn't fathom having to go home and tell all my family and friends who had supported me, who had never told me I was crazy for thinking this was a good idea, that I had failed and didn't have what it took to succeed.

So instead of running back home where I felt safe, warm, and loved, I stayed. In the past, I had been guilty of running from my pain. I would ignore it, hope it would go away, or completely deny it. By staying right where I was, I had no choice but to sit with the pain, the frustration, the exhaustion, the fear, and the multitude of other stuffed emotions that were finally coming up.

I let the emotions slowly move from a full boil to a simmer. I cried more tears with my sisters and shared that I was tired, overwhelmed, and completely unsure where I was headed in my life. I knew I was ready for a change, that the life I had left behind was no longer what I wanted, and that my daily commutes, long hours, never-ending emails, and unfulfilling job were tearing me apart.

That weekend, I realized that I was having a life-changing experience. The teachers had warned us about this during that first evening together. Once I began to do this work and rediscover what my soul wanted and needed, I began to slowly unravel the threads of my life I had woven over the years. I was uncovering what was hidden beneath and reclaiming what was important to me, and I knew there was no going back.

Like any roller coaster ride, there are still ups and downs after that first big fall. I didn't come home from that weekend knowing exactly what I needed to do, but I did know that I was on the path and that I had to trust the process. I had to trust my inner voice, let go of the fear that was keeping me from embracing change, and have the courage to step into the unknown.

Often, before the breakthrough comes the breakdown. Some of our most challenging experiences provide us with the insight to move forward in a new direction. The breakdown is never fun, but sometimes it is necessary. It takes courage to keep moving forward and a resilient spirit to pave the way.

CHAPTER 13

The Evolution

"If one advances confidently in the direction of his dreams, and endeavors to live the life which he has imagined, he will meet with a success unexpected in common hours."

—*Henry David Thoreau*

Each time I returned from my teacher training weekend, it became harder and harder to get back into the swing of things at home and work. Every time I came home, I was a slightly different person, and it took time to let the new me assimilate. Although I had proclaimed during the first weekend of the training that I didn't intend to teach at all, I was starting to feel like I wanted to share my experiences and the power of these practices.

I was beginning to recognize that I could start where I was by helping others in the corporate environment. I could teach my colleagues (those interested, anyway) how to breathe, how to reconnect with their bodies, how to live from their hearts and not just their minds.

I realized that it was no longer my dream to reach the top rung of the corporate ladder but instead to teach others that they have a well of wisdom within them, that they can stop chasing what they think they need to achieve to feel successful, that success can't be defined by our titles or how much money we make, and that within every one of us we have unconditional and unlimited peace and love available all the time.

I wanted more than anything to bring authenticity to the conference rooms, to help my colleagues begin to truly see one another, and to give them the courage to dream big and trust that they had the support of something greater than them. I still couldn't pinpoint what exactly that thing was, but I had a renewed faith that it didn't matter what we called it as long as we believed in it, trusted it, and knew that it was guiding us on our path.

I also knew that these concepts were somewhat new to the corporate world and were, in many cases, unwelcome. Yet I believed it to be a worthy endeavor. If the things that I had learned could help others manage their stress, find more joy in their lives, and be more authentic, I was up for the task.

I understood that some people would embrace yoga and mindfulness while others would think these practices were crazy. I decided to start with the one and only thing I could control: myself.

I made a pact with myself to be more authentic at work. I wanted to be more real and open with my bosses, my employees, and my peers. I no longer thought it was necessary or meaningful to separate the person who I was at home with the person I was at work. I wanted to be true to who I was, regardless of where I was or who I was with. I wanted to be more vulnerable. To let people see the real me, blemishes and all. It was my hope that by showing up in this way, others would be inspired to lead with more compassion and realness, as well.

I began to use breathing exercises as I was walking from my office to conference rooms so that I was more calm, relaxed, and present during meetings.

Have you ever noticed how many people have their heads in their laptops answering emails during work meetings? I challenge you to shut your laptop (or even leave it at your desk), put your phone down, and give your full attention to the meeting you are actually in. You might be amazed at how much more productive you are and how much more you accomplish. Once you experience the benefits of being mindful during a meeting, you might even begin to ask others to follow your lead.

After noticing the effects of being more present in my interactions with colleagues, I started to notice my mindset also shifting. I noticed their strengths more readily and became less focused on their weaknesses. I could witness conversations that were occurring with neutrality, without getting emotional or frustrated.

I realized that my ability to be more aware of my thoughts created a space between when my brain received information and when I responded. I had learned to pause and process before reacting, and this allowed me to respond from a more centered and productive place.

I took more breaks from my computer to move, stretch, and reconnect with my body. I tried to eat meals away from my desk, taking the time to encourage others to do the same and share a meal.

These are all small and easy things that you can start to do. You don't need to add more items to your to-do list or hours to your day. Instead, simply start by picking one of the exercises below to incorporate into your week. Then, next week, choose another. And another. You might be surprised by the impact that these have over a few weeks or months.

- Take a few deep breaths as you walk to your next meeting

- Notice what you see, hear, taste, feel, and smell

- Stretch at your desk or get up and move around

- Pay attention to your thoughts and reactions

- Shut your laptop, put your phone away, and be present in meetings and during conversations

- Eat lunch away from your desk

- Look for others' strengths instead of focusing solely on weaknesses

- Pause—then respond.

These were all small things that I hoped would not only improve my levels of stress and overall health but also show others that it was OK to practice self-care and that it could be helpful even in these small ways. Workplace wellness can mean a lot of different things, but for me it was finding ways to still live my yoga at work.

There were many unanticipated benefits. I received more smiles from people as I took the time to say good morning or simply make eye contact in the hallways. People who didn't work for me and whom I didn't know well asked me to be their mentor. My bosses began to assign me projects that were more in line with what I was passionate about and wanted to work on.

I was sending out a different energy than I'd had in the past, and the response was immediate and undeniable. The positivity I was projecting was coming back to me in ways I hadn't experienced before. Without necessarily trying, my work life began to align a little bit more, and I no longer felt I was living two separate lives. I was embracing who I was, all of me, and was witnessing an acceptance and even appreciation from those around me.

I later realized that there were other corporate junkies finding success in bringing authenticity and mindfulness into the workplace. Janice Marturano, a former General Mills executive, founded the Institute for Mindful Leadership after witnessing firsthand the benefits of mindfulness in her career. Her award-winning book *Finding the Space to Lead: A Practical Guide for Mindful Leadership* is now required reading in several university business school programs[18].

Bill George, a Harvard Business School professor and former CEO of Medtronic, credits meditation as the single most important thing that he has done over the years to improve his leadership[19]. In his bestselling book *Discover Your True North,* he shares how meditation and compassion practices can make better and more authentic leaders.

For his book, he interviewed almost two hundred leaders in the business world, including Warren Buffet, Mark Zuckerberg, and Arianna Huffington. His interviews and studies resulted in transformational exercises on how to be the leader you want to be. He undoubtedly helped to bring more purpose and soul into the corporate world as leaders learned from him how to discover their true north and then stay faithful to it in their leadership roles.

Slowly but surely, executives across the world are beginning to embrace the tenets of mindfulness and are finding ways to better manage their stress and become more focused and productive at work. They are also learning that, in addition to reducing their own stress, mindfulness can positively impact their company's bottom line.

The annual cost to employers for stress-related healthcare is estimated at around 300 billion dollars annually, largely due to missed work and loss of productivity. In fact, 40 percent of employee turnover is directly related to stress[20]. The impacts of stress on the business world are so great that leaders can't afford not to pay attention to stress-reducing practices like yoga, meditation, and self-care.

CHAPTER 14

On the Path

"Your life is a sacred journey. It is about change, growth, discovery, movement, transformation, continuously expanding your vision of what is possible, stretching your soul, learning to see clearly and deeply, listening to your intuition, taking courageous challenges at every step along the way . . . You are on the path, exactly where you are meant to be right now . . . And from here, you can only go forward, shaping your life story into a magnificent tale of triumph, of healing, of courage, of beauty, of wisdom, of power, of dignity, and of love."

—*Caroline Adams*

During the weeks leading up to my final weekend of teacher training, every spare moment was filled with yoga. I was studying the concepts and was trying to find my voice as a teacher. I was struggling with my newfound identity as a yogi. Despite getting ready for graduation and preparing to enter into this new world as a yoga teacher, I was facing insecurities around this new me.

I was changing. Evolving. Growing. Expanding. And it was scary. I was worried about what others thought of me. I didn't think anyone would see me as a yogi. I was feeling like a fake, a fraud.

I later realized that these were growing pains. We often feel the tug-of-war between our former selves and our new selves as we shed our layers. The new us doesn't become that beautiful butterfly overnight; it takes time and effort.

Part of that effort is in embracing the new you and accepting who you are without needing acceptance from others.

Have you ever known something was right for you but still questioned it based on what others would think? Of course you have. I'm certain it's a universal experience. We want people to like us and we want people to agree with us. It feels good to have people support and cheer us on.

Sometimes, however, you need to be your own biggest cheerleader. You can't always depend on others to know the right path for you. You alone are responsible for your life and the paths that you take. Trusting that inner voice and doing what is right for you, despite what others think, will steer you in the right direction.

On our final weekend, I knew I was in the right place. I could feel the apprehension, nervousness, and excitement in the air. Our teachers knew we were still reeling from the scolding the last time we were together, so they gave us a pep talk to help ease our worry and inflate our confidence.

They told us that we were right where we were supposed to be and that they had faith in us. We had learned what we needed to and should trust that we were ready. Looking around, I knew that we were. We had all slowly unfolded over our time together. Like lotus flowers that grow from the mud and muck, we had found our way to the surface to grow into our individual beauty.

We were all unique and very different from one another, but our common bond was that we had been willing to be vulnerable. We had laughed, cried, and shared our innermost selves with one another. That vulnerability allowed us to truly see one another as well as ourselves. It taught us that we all had fears. We all shared hopes and dreams. Together we recognized that, at our core, we were all the same.

That togetherness allowed us to witness our growth and celebrate transformation. The ability to be authentically real helped us evolve past what we had originally anticipated for ourselves and become so much more.

The support from my sangha sisters was palpable in the air. Despite our nerves as we waited for our final exam, we made small talk, tried to relax, and continued to support one another.

When it was finally my turn to meet with our teachers, I nervously walked into the room and sat down in front of them. We exchanged pleasantries, and then they got right to work. They began to ask me questions: Where did yoga originally come from? What does the word *yoga* mean? Name the various styles of yoga. My analytical brain kicked into overdrive, and I regurgitated all the necessary details from my studies to pass their test.

As I reflect back on those moments, I realize that what I wanted to tell my teachers was that I didn't really care where yoga came from or what styles we practiced in the US. I wanted to tell them that yoga had changed my life. I wanted to claim my new identity as a recovering corporate junkie and a yogi.

I wanted to explain that, through the practices, they taught me to find myself again. It was the part of me I had long ago hidden from because I didn't think it was what others wanted to see. I didn't think it was the part of me that was going to help me get ahead in life and prove to others that I was worthy—worthy of success, worthy of love, worthy enough to be truly seen. All of me.

Instead, I simply thanked them and shared how incredibly grateful I was for the experience and for their support. As I left that room, I knew I was embarking on a new adventure—an adventure that would undoubtedly take my life in a new and more meaningful direction. I wasn't exactly sure yet what it would look like, but I had faith in the journey and I knew that I would figure it out along the way.

After that weekend I knew wholeheartedly that I was on the right path. I had a renewed confidence that I would become a teacher and share with others what I had learned so that they too could experience, even if just for a fleeting moment, what it was like to be still, quiet, without worry, and completely at ease. I decided that to teach others how to reunite with their natural state of being would be true success and the highlight of my career.

Can I look back and confidently say I uncovered the recipe to yoga's secret sauce and found enlightenment? No, not necessarily, but what I found was better. I rediscovered the depth of my soul. I created deeper and more meaningful relationships. I found inspiration in surprising places and saw beauty around me like I'd never experienced before.

That is my wish for you. My hope is that by sharing my story, you too will be able to use these tools to experience a glimpse of quiet contentment, the feeling of overwhelming gratitude, and a trust that you are right where you are supposed to be on your path and journey through life.

PART 2

Transformation

Going from a corporate junkie who was stressed to the max and constantly worried about what everyone else thought of her to a more relaxed and peaceful person who embraced who she was didn't happen overnight. In fact, there are days that I still struggle with my identity and with not needing everyone's approval. There are days where I let the demands of my life get the best of me and I lose my cool.

Most days, however, I can witness those experiences of my life and see them more clearly for what they are. You might think I'm crazy, but I literally talk to myself. I say things like:

"There you go feeling stressed out again."
"You are feeling tired, angry, frustrated."
"You feel as if you need that person to like you."
"Nicole, you are upset because you think . . ."

The difference between the way that I think now and how I used to think is that I now realize that I am not my thoughts. I allow myself instead to witness my thoughts and see them for what they are.

A few years ago my husband and I were going through couples' counseling and learned a new way of communicating with each other. As we talked with our therapist and shared our frustrations about what we thought the other person meant when they said or did something, she helped us understand that what we were thinking was not always the reality. She taught us to say, "The story that I made up in my head is . . ."

When we needed to clarify a situation with one another, we would begin with this phrase. (Full disclosure: My husband was way better at this than me. I still want to believe the stories in my head and prove him wrong. I'm still working on this one.)

What I've learned over years of witnessing the fluctuations of my mind is that we don't need to attach meaning to our thoughts. We can simply acknowledge them for what they are: just thoughts. They do not define us or make us who we are. The real us is at our core, in our center, not in our minds.

One of the yoga teachers I've had the privilege to take classes from often says exactly that during his class. He reminds us that all that we are and everything we need is within us. Whether we are looking for strength, cour-age, peace, love, compassion, or anything else, it is always there for us. We just need to learn to see it.

The second part of this book will help you to do that. Through the questions and exercises in each section my hope is that you learn how to see the true and beautiful you. The you that knows enlightenment is within reach and is always available. The you that is waiting to be uncovered and ready to welcome you back home.

CHAPTER 15

The Cycle of Life

"Life is made up of a collection of moments that are not ours to keep. The pain we encounter throughout our days spent on this earth comes from the illusion that some moments can be held onto. Clinging to people and experiences that were never ours in the first place is what causes us to miss out on the beauty of the miracle that is the now. All of this is yours, yet none of it is. How could it be? Look around you. Everything is fleeting."

—*Rachel Brathen*

This morning I decided to go for a walk. It's the first part of November in Minnesota, which typically means it's freezing cold outside, windy and unbearable. Fortunately, today was the opposite of that; the air was brisk but the sun was warm and inviting. I was feeling somewhat melancholy as I headed outside but knew, from my own experience, that the fresh air and gentle movement of my body would help me feel better.

Before I got even three blocks from my home, I felt tears begin to well up in my eyes. In the past I would have held the tears back—what kind of crazy woman cries while she's walking down the street?—and forced myself to get a grip. Instead I found my inner self talking to me with the care of a nurturing mom soothing a teary child. I heard the words, "It's OK, just let it out."

I wanted to trace the tears and find out exactly where they were coming from and why I was feeling this way, but I couldn't pinpoint it. I heard that nurturing voice again, saying, "You don't have to know why or where they are coming from. Just let the tears move through you and let go."

As I heard this, I looked around me and began to see with fresh eyes. Things slowly began to make more sense. I could see transition and transformation happening all around me. There were trees that still held onto their fall leaves with beautiful colors of gold, orange, and vibrant red. There were trees that were completely barren and looked like they were dead. There were also trees that were still green and looked like no change had happened to them over the fall season. Through all of this, the sun was shining brightly and bringing nourishment and light to all the trees, regardless of their stage.

What I realized in this moment was that my tears were simply a part of the cycle of life.

There are times in my life when I have remained stagnant and held onto things, wanting them to remain just as they were without allowing for any change. But as I've become more in tune with my inner world and my needs, I've had to shed my old thoughts and patterns, which has often left me feeling barren.

As I released my old ways, I felt lonely and uncertain about who I was becoming. Just like the empty trees that were sitting among the beauty, all alone, I felt as if I were in a world to myself. But through trial and tribulation, what I've come to learn is that there is always growth after the darkness. The transformation is silently and invisibly occurring, even though it looks as if you are lifeless on the outside.

The most brilliant changes occur only if you stay with them long enough for a rebirth. As you allow the inner world to speak to you, the unfolding slowly takes place, like a thousand-petal lotus flower opening. Your unfolding, like the lotus or the trees, can bring a beauty you have not yet had the opportunity to witness. The new you is changed. You are different than you were before but in the most brilliant and fitting of ways.

My yoga practice has taught me that we are a part of the cycle of the earth. We are the cycle of life, and there is no separation between us and all the other particles of energy and life force in the universe. We lose sight of this as we learn and are enculturated to hide our emotions and disconnect from our inner guidance. As we relearn how to listen—not to our thoughts, but to our true essence, our true self—we begin to realize that change and growth are inevitable. We have three options when faced with our inner growth: we can accept it, embrace it, or fight it.

When we refuse to allow the cycle of life, the ups and downs, to move through us and change us, we refuse to allow our best selves to be seen. While you are going through all this, you are constantly enveloped in a bright light of love and compassion. The universe, God, or whatever you choose to call the greater power is always there to warm you on the coldest of days.

My walk ended at my daughter's school. I had signed up to volunteer in her kindergarten classroom. As I walked into the room, I could feel the excitable energy and happiness of the kids. At their young age, many of the kids haven't yet fully embraced the lessons our society had taught them regarding their feelings and emotions.

Just watch a young child for a while and you will surely agree. Their emotions have incredible peaks and valleys, and they experience them with unbelievable vigor. When they are happy, you can see their smile from ear to ear and feel their joy. If you look into their eyes, you can almost see that they are smiling from their soul. On the flip side, when they are sad, angry, frustrated, or hurt, they let you know with their tears and voice. They may not have the words yet to fully express themselves verbally, but there is no question what they are feeling.

What would it be like if adults allowed themselves to express all their feelings and emotions as openly as our children do? It might cause some uncomfortable conversations and raw emotions but would bring with them some heartfelt words.

Instead of stuffing our thoughts and feelings, we would be able to experience more growth and transformation. We would be living from a place more in tune with the cycle of our life and would respectfully listen to our inner selves. We would no longer question if we were doing the right or wrong thing because we would only do what was right by our spirit. We would no longer make decisions to please others but would be instead concerned about what was right for ourselves.

What would it look like if you began to speak your truth in a loving and compassionate way? Would your life begin to slowly unfold in new ways? Would you feel a sense of relief for finally allowing yourself to freely express your thoughts, emotions, and needs? I challenge you to give it a try.

My yoga practice hasn't cured me from all the pain and inevitable suffering of life. What it has done is provide me with a safe and nurturing way to experience difficult emotions. What I used to stuff inside of me now has a way to come to the surface. My emotions now have an avenue for expression so that they don't continue to sit within me, causing dis-ease.

The true strength of the soul becomes visible when someone is brave enough to sit with the pain, breathe through it, and come out on the other side having felt, experienced, and conquered it.

Buddhist nun and American philosopher Pema Chödrön summed this up beautifully when she said, "So even if the hot loneliness is there, and for 1.6 seconds we sit with that restlessness when yesterday we couldn't sit for even one, that's the journey of the warrior."[21]

Our yoga practice teaches us the journey of the warrior. It's our choice whether we are brave enough to step into the journey and battle through. As with any battle, you can give up and give in to the struggle, or you can fight through it and become that much stronger and more resilient on the other side.

Suffering may be universal and inevitable, but we can learn to lessen our burden and move through the most challenging of times if we are brave enough to face the truth.

JOURNAL EXERCISE:

Take some time to contemplate the following questions and write your reactions to them. Try to allow the responses to flow freely, without overthinking or holding back.

Where in your life are you not speaking your truth?

What is keeping you from being honest and open?

How can you begin to be more truthful to yourself and others?

Can you freely express your thoughts, emotions, and needs? If not, why not?

How does it feel to speak freely, with compassion and integrity?

CHAPTER 16

Highs and Lows

"The simple things are also the most extraordinary things, and only the wise can see them."

—*Paulo Coelho*

My kids recently convinced me to buy them the newest trend going around the elementary school (yes, apparently trends in elementary school exist). They had been to a friend's house who had a special beaded bracelet that was all the rage.

All I knew from my kids was that the beads were somehow filled with water and mud. It sounded strange, so I was intrigued and wanted to learn more. When we finally found them at the checkout desk as we were getting ready to leave the store, the cashier explained to me that the beads have water in them from Mt. Everest, the highest place in the world, and mud from the Dead Sea, the lowest place in the world.

She went on to explain that the bracelet was supposed to be used as a daily reminder that there is balance in the world. Some days you are on top and need to be reminded to stay humble. Other days you have hit the bottom and need help being hopeful.

The company that sells them, Lokai, explains on their website that life is a journey, and we are always fluctuating in between the highs and lows.

I really didn't expect to be getting a lesson on the journey of life and finding balance when I went out in search of these bracelets. But I was certainly glad that I did. It provided me with an opportunity to talk with my kids about our journey through life and how there would be times when they felt like absolutely nothing was going their way. There would also be times when they felt like there is no challenge they couldn't handle. The important part was to always remember that we could ride the wave, the highs and the lows, with steadiness and grace.

We have within us the steadfast ability to hold on through the ups and downs. We have an ability to feel the ecstasy and joy that come in fleeting moments and to feel the heartache and sadness that linger at times. Not only can we handle the emotions, but we can recognize that within the darkness or joy we have an inner light that shines steadily, regardless of how our emotional body is feeling.

We are not our emotions. We are not what happens to us or the highs and lows that we experience. We are something greater than that and can tap into that place of steady light even as we are surrounded by darkness. Every time we come to our mats, we are reminded that we can be humble and hopeful. We can choose to shine bright and choose happiness, despite any external forces telling us we should do otherwise.

How many people have you met who constantly choose to focus on the darkness? Instead of seeing each experience as unique and recognizing it for what it is, they dwell on the times they have experienced a low. They choose to hold on for dear life and even begin to define themselves by this experience.

The same sometimes goes for people who have had some incredibly high and exciting moments that they believe now define them. We have all met those people as well. Every time you see them, they share the same stories over and over. They can't seem to let go of the experience they had to open themselves up for the present or future. By dwelling on the past, they can't ride the waves of their current experiences to embrace the good, the bad, and the everything in between.

We can choose which story we want to live and how we want to define our lives. Knowing that not every moment is going to be full of ecstasy allows us to appreciate it more when it is present. Knowing that not every moment is going to feel hopeless helps us to sit with it when it's present. The majority of our life isn't lived at the top of Mt. Everest or the bottom of the Dead Sea. Most of our life is lived in the sweet, subtle moments in between.

JOURNAL EXERCISE:

Take some time to contemplate the following questions and write your reactions to them. Try to allow the responses to flow freely, without overthinking or holding back.

What do you want the story of your life to be? Which stories are you ready to let go of so that you can stand more fully in your authentic self?

Are you ready to shift your mindset and begin to be more open to the present moment? Can you begin to embrace the subtle sweetness of life without constantly striving to reach the top of the mountain?

CHAPTER 17
Finding Contentment

"Happiness is when what you think, what you say, and what you do are in harmony."

—*Mahatma Gandhi*

If you're not careful, striving and stress can follow you wherever you go, even if you begin to make some of the changes we've been talking about throughout this book. I have experienced this firsthand. My desire for success persisted even as I was shifting gears and leaving the corporate world.

I had learned that my yoga teacher was selling the studio I had made my home, so I decided that buying it would be the perfect transition from the corporate world and into the wellness world. As I went through the decision to become a business owner and stepped into that role, I slowly began to realize that I was feeling the same kind of stress that I had during my cubicle days.

I wanted to dive fully into ownership of the yoga studio, to turn it from where it was to a thriving and profitable business. I wanted to prove myself and earn the respect of sangha sisters, coworkers, friends, and family.

In my efforts to win everyone over and my striving for a new version of success, I was creating unnecessary stress for myself. I had left the confines of the corporate world for flexibility, ease, and freedom. Yet here I was causing myself to feel overwhelmed, overworked, and time-strapped. I had no one to blame this time but myself.

One of the niyamas I obviously needed to work on, but didn't realize at the time, was santosha. Santosha is a Sanskrit word meaning contentment. It means being satisfied in the present moment without the desire for things to be different. It is accepting what is instead of wanting for what isn't.

As I think back to the first few months of transitioning out of the corporate world and into owning a yoga studio, I realize that practicing santosha is one of my biggest growth opportunities (as only a corporate junkie can say). I was reaching so much for what I thought I should be accomplishing that I wasn't able to just appreciate and enjoy what I did have. I was constantly striving to do more, to be more, more, more, more.

Coming from the corporate world, I can understand why the concept of contentment seemed to be so challenging.

Our work culture teaches us that we are never enough and that we've never done enough. When we complete a project, we typically don't even take the time to celebrate before we move on to the next thing. When we finally get that promotion we've worked so hard for, we start working on what we need to do to get to the next one—or at least our next raise.

We learn that staying in one job or position for any length of time shows complacency and a lack of motivation and determination. Instead we are taught to constantly lean in to and give our all so that we can constantly move up the ladder.

Think about Sheryl Sandberg's highly acclaimed book *Lean In*[22]. It reinforced the idea that women should put their all into their family life, their work life, their everything. I used to support this idea. The old me leaned in as much as she could all day, every day. That was before I learned there was another option and that I didn't have to keep pushing myself to do it all.

Following Sheryl's fame as the COO of Facebook and the youngest woman on the *Forbes* list of the fifty most powerful women in business, she experienced the unexpected and traumatic death of her husband. She writes about her experience and how her life changed abruptly in *Option B: Facing Adversity, Building Resilience, and Finding Joy*[23].

Her *lean in* mentality changed as she suddenly found herself overwhelmed with grief and unable to function with the same level of ease and drive that she had before. She had to dig deep to find the energy to get dressed for the day or to sit through a meeting at work. Instead of putting all her energy into the tasks and responsibilities around her, she found herself having to focus all of her energy on simply being.

She experienced traumatic stress firsthand and realized that she no longer could lean into all aspects of her life the way she had originally believed was paramount to being a successful businesswoman.

She shares in her second book how she was no longer able to contribute in meetings the way she had in the past. But instead of beating herself up for saying the wrong thing or being unable to add insight or direction, she was learning to be grateful that she was able to contribute at all. Her boss, Mark Zuckerberg, taught her to look for the positive and commended her for what she was able to bring instead of holding her to the same expectations she had of herself and being disappointed by what she couldn't do.

She learned the hard way to practice self-care, which could be more accurately defined as self-preservation in light of the difficult times she was going through. Her ability to be resilient and to ultimately experience moments of joy again was tied to her willingness to honor where she was—body, mind, and spirit—and what she was going through. Had she forced herself to continue to lean into life the way she had, she wouldn't have had the chance to move through her trauma and experience the posttraumatic growth that she did.

Another highly acclaimed businesswoman and author has used her experience with stress and trauma to share with others how they could find growth as well. Arianna Huffington, the cofounder and original editor in chief of the *Huffington Post*, talks about her experience with adrenal fatigue in her book *Thrive*[24]. In her quest to not just reach the top but to continuously, day after day, stay at the top, she wore her body out.

One day, after passing out from exhaustion, she woke up with a broken jaw and bloody head. After many tests in the doctor's office to find out what horrible ailment caused her to fall, she found out she was just worn out. She was tired. The pace of her life and lack of self-care practices had hindered her health so much so that her body gave out.

This story isn't all that unfamiliar if we really think about it. We learn at a young age to continually strive for more; to be faster, better, and smarter; and to push ourselves to our limits. I remember being encouraged to stay up late to study for tests so that I could get good grades, get into college, and ultimately succeed in life.

In high school, I worked my body to exhaustion during the cross-country running season because it was the only way I would ever make the varsity team. I remember getting mononucleosis during middle school because I had pushed myself so hard for so long. What I don't remember is anyone ever telling me to slow down or honor what my body was telling me, or teaching me how to do so.

In our desire to get ahead in life, we are losing sight of self-care and santosha. If we could learn to go to bed at night appreciative for our accomplishments of the day instead of thinking about all that we didn't get done or need to do the next day, we might learn to lessen our stress, anxiety, and overwhelm. Instead of constantly striving for more, what could our lives look like if we learned to surrender and accept what was?

It has taken a lot of work and surrendering on my part, but I'm slowly beginning to embrace this practice. I became used to asking myself at the end of the day if I was happy with what I had achieved. That was instilled in me at a very young age and throughout my years of being a corporate junkie. My inner dialogue is slowly starting to shift to where I am more concerned with being satisfied, or at least content, with who I am, where I am, and faith that I am right where I am supposed to be. Now, I'm beginning to ask myself, "Am I happy with who I was in the world today?"

Do you constantly find yourself striving to do more and be more? Are there areas in your life where you can begin to embrace the idea of contentment?

Can you end the day feeling happy for who you were instead of what you did? Can you honor the needs of your body, mind, and spirit instead of your ego?

What would it feel like if you allowed contentment to filter into your life a little bit, instead of constantly striving for more?

CHAPTER 18

Experiencing Enlightenment

"Knowing others is wisdom; knowing the self is enlightenment.
Mastering others requires force; mastering the self needs strength."

—*Lao Tzu*

Throughout my journey after finding yoga, I was still in search of the long-lasting and elusive state of enlightenment. I had read about it in my yoga texts, studied the sutras, and deliberately come back to my mat time and time again. Still, I wasn't living in a constant state of bliss. I didn't quite understand how to accomplish what I envisioned as the ultimate state of euphoria, where there were no struggles, no pain, and no suffering.

Enlightenment can be defined in many ways, but the one that I was clinging to was the idea that you could be in a state in which you lacked both desire and suffering. But the first precept of Buddhism is that suffering is universal, so how could we possibly reach enlightenment? If everyone is inevitably suffering, it must have been some kind of cruel joke.

Isn't desire a part of life? Is it truly wrong to desire and want something bigger, better, or more meaningful for your life? As I continued to question this, I dug deeper and decided to inquire with the masters by googling enlightenment, looking for a solid definition. What I found was a big list of very vague definitions that differed tremendously by source.

What I finally landed on was the only definition that resonated with me: "the condition of being informed spiritually." I could reason with that. As I came to my mat and found that quiet place within me, I felt connected to and informed by spirit. Before finding yoga, I felt a lack of spirituality and didn't feel like I was being guided by anything but my brain and, periodically, my heart. Through my yoga, I learned how to tune into my inner guidance, my spirit, so that I was making choices about my life and living from a more informed place.

If you take it a bit further and break apart the word enlightenment, you find the word "lighten." Without having to ask the experts (aka Google), I knew that to lighten can be to become brighter, to lessen your load, and to become less dark.

When I first starting practicing yoga and experienced that moment of bliss, I came back to my mat time and time again, searching for those moments when my world was lighter and brighter and there was less darkness. In fact, if I am being honest with myself, that's the underlying desire and motivation for everything I do. Who doesn't want to live in a world that is full of light, love, happiness, and joy?

JOURNAL EXERCISE:

Take some time to contemplate the following questions and write your reactions to them. Try to allow the responses to flow freely, without overthinking or holding back.

Have you experienced a glimpse of what might be enlightenment? How do you experience it? What does it look like and feel like, for you?

Do you have practices that help to inform you spiritually? Can you take breaks from listening to your mind and connect more fully with your inner guidance?

What messages do you hear when you do slow down enough to connect with your whole self? What would it take for you to feel more love, light, happiness, and joy in your life?

CHAPTER 19

Still Learning

"No one is wise by birth, for wisdom results from one's efforts."

—*T. Krishnamacharya*

Even after years of studying and teaching yoga, I'm still working every day to live the practices, recognize my lessons, and embrace the process. I know that I'm on a journey, that there is a bigger plan for me, and that the universe has my back. I'm continuously working to cultivate the blind trust that I need every single day to move through the challenges with ease.

A CEO I worked for used to help his employees navigate change and know where to focus our energies by using the analogy of a big field. In Minnesota, we are surrounded by rural farms where many of us spent time during our youth working. One of the jobs was to be a "rock picker." They were responsible for combing the fields for big rocks and removing them so that the tractors wouldn't get stuck or be damaged. The farmers would tell the rock pickers not to worry about the little rocks that were all over the field but instead to focus on the big rocks.

For over a year, my CEO used that analogy to help us focus our institution's big issues. It helped us to let go of the smaller worries and spend our time and energy on what was most important.

This analogy can be translated to our minds and the big and small thoughts that we have running through them all day long. In yoga philosophy, we call this chitta vritti. The little rocks are the pesky thoughts that tend to ruminate and keep us distracted and preoccupied throughout the day. The big rocks can disrupt our path until we remove them from our presence. We then continue on, witnessing and becoming overwhelmed by the pesky little reminders that we can't get away from.

Mindfulness allows us to see the rocks so that we can make an informed choice to respond to them or not and continue to move forward on our path. When we are being mindful, we are living in the present moment, aware of what is happening within us and around us. We are experiencing life without placing judgment or letting the chitta vritti take over. We allow our experience to unfold so that we can respond to situations in a nonreactive way.

As we are faced with major life challenges—big rocks— we have the ability to face them without relinquishing our power. When we come up against the little rocks, those pesky and unrelenting bumps in the road, we can't allow them to affect our journey or our spirit. If we aren't moving forward in a mindful way, the rocks we meet may cause us to break down.

That's what happened with Dan Harris, a TV journalist and the author of *10% Happier*[25]. In his book, he tells the story of an on-air panic attack and what led up to it. As he quickly climbed the ladder in his chosen pro- fession, he learned that in order to beat the competition and be recognized as a legitimate reporter he had to work nonstop and travel across the world without tak- ing a moment's break. Following his panic attack, he was forced to learn self-care and how to slow down. In his search for a remedy, he found that meditation was the most effective way to quiet his inner voice, calm his body, and reduce stress.

He admits that the changes he has made haven't led him to a life free of stress and suffering, but that overall he is 10 percent happier than he used to be. That means he has around two and a half more enjoyable hours each day.

How many of us have worked ourselves to the point of a panic attack or meltdown? How many of us have—in our desire to achieve, to succeed, to matter—worked our- selves to complete exhaustion? I have.

When my husband was deployed to Iraq, my hair started to fall out in clumps. I literally had handfuls of hair coming out at a time. I remember asking my hairdresser why it was happening, thinking it must be the cheap brand of shampoo I was using or the heat from my straightener. When she didn't have an answer, I began to worry that I must be sick and plagued with an awful disease. The chitta vritti in my mind took over and I was constantly worried about my demise. When my doctor confirmed there was nothing seriously wrong with me, I was relieved but also shocked.

Never did it cross my mind that it was stress. I hadn't realized that my worry, my overdoing and trying to prove myself by achieving and handling everything on my own, could be causing my hair to fall out. Nor did I want to admit that I couldn't handle it.

Not only can meditation help you recognize the big and small rocks in your life, but it can also provide you with a helpful tool for navigating them. By learning to slow down the constant fluctuations of the mind, you can begin to shift your relationship to stress.

You will still have stress, but you can loosen its grip on your life. Meditation, whether you are practicing mindfulness or another form, can retrain your brain so that your thoughts don't take over and thrust you into the fight, flight, or freeze state we've already discussed. You will likely experience the ability to maneuver through your days with more ease, less reactivity, and better overall health.

MEDITATION PRACTICE:

- Set a timer on your phone for two minutes

- Find a comfortable seat and close your eyes

- For the full two minutes until your timer goes off, just notice your thoughts and the fluctuations of your mind

JOURNAL EXERCISE:

Take some time to contemplate the following questions and write your reactions to them. Try to allow the responses to flow freely, without overthinking or holding back.

Was your mind moving from thought to thought to thought? Did you have any pauses between your thoughts where your mind was quiet?

Did you notice a theme to your thoughts or were they all over the board? Were you surprised by what you noticed?

Did two minutes go by quickly or did you feel like the timer would never go off?

CHAPTER 20

Mindful Moments

"You can't stop the waves, but you can learn to surf."

—*Jon Kabat-Zinn*

Everything seems sweeter when you are on vacation. The breeze feels calmer, the flowers look and smell more vibrant. The sounds of the waves, the birds, the chattering of little kids and families as they play on the beach. The taste of the pineapple ice cream as it melts on your tongue and the cool stickiness drips down your chin. Every moment of togetherness feels like a gift. The busyness of our daily lives melts away as we slowly begin to witness, experience, and appreciate the moments of our days.

As I write this, I'm sitting on a lounge chair in Mexico reflecting on the past several years. I realize, with a heart full of gratitude, that all my days have become sweeter since I embarked on this journey.

Even on my busy days, as I'm running around with my kids and managing a business and a full life, my moments have become more joy-filled. I'm still stressed at times. I still strive to achieve and to be a competent mom, teacher, friend, and spouse. But I am more awake. I notice a sweet smile from my daughter and the importance of that after-school hug from my son. I enjoy a glimpse out the windows and the sparkling of the sun on the snow.

I also take less time than ever before beating myself up or worrying about things that don't matter—like what other people think about me.

It seems I've finally embodied mindfulness.

Mindfulness is defined by Jon Kabat-Zinn as "paying attention to the present moment without judgment."[25] In other words, allow yourself to be awake and aware in every moment without letting the inner gremlins try to put value or place judgment on it.

Our brains are constantly talking to us, telling us what we should accept and what we shouldn't. Santosha teaches us that we can instead choose to be ambivalent, that we don't have to find meaning in every experience. We can simply allow for the experience to happen, bring our awareness to it as it's happening, and accept it.

A yoga student of mine always leaves my class by looking me in the eye and saying, "Have mindful moments." I love this. If you read into this simple phrase, you might believe, as I do, that he is saying, "I know life isn't perfect and every second of each day isn't filled with rainbows and butterflies, but try to embrace some of the moments to truly appreciate them and love them for what they are."

Living in the present moment is just that: taking moments throughout the day to be aware of everything that is happening around you and within you. You can let everything else become a dim light in the distance as you feel and experience what is.

Mindfulness meditations and present-moment awareness practices help us to pause the busyness of our lives, if only for a moment, to truly see all that is around and within us. They help us shift our perspective to appreciation and gratitude as we see with renewed eyes. It helps us become more aware so that we can tune in to the more subtle occurrences happening around us all the time.

Have you ever noticed how, when you walk into a room after someone has gotten into an argument, it feels heavy? The air feels thick, and you know, intuitively, that something isn't right. Now imagine you walk into a room after someone has just won the lottery or gotten engaged. You can feel that the air is light and the energy in the room is celebratory and happy before you even know what has happened.

We can shift our energy and the way that others see and experience us by choosing the light instead of the darkness. If you are a corporate junkie early on in your path and don't yet have the courage to make a career change—or aren't even sure you want to—think about how you can choose to be the light. How can you make your days lighter, more meaningful, and more connected to who you are instead of who you think you should be?

You know those people who always seem to have things fall into place for them? Who don't seem to share your struggles in life? I can promise you that they do struggle and that their lives aren't nearly as perfect as you believe them to be from the outside. They've just learned to shift their perspective and, quite possibly, their energy. They've likely learned to embrace mindfulness as well so that they can be present in the moment without all the unnecessary judgment and baggage we bring to the table.

Like anything, the more we practice mindfulness, the more it becomes our second nature. Coming back to being mindful, moment to moment, will change you. Before you know it, you might be moving through life with greater grace, appreciation, and joy.

JOURNAL EXERCISE:

Take some time to contemplate the following questions and write your reactions to them. Try to allow the responses to flow freely, without overthinking or holding back.

How often throughout your day do you think you are fully present?

What kind of energy do you notice around you and what kind of energy do you think you are putting out into the world?

Do you tend to walk around your problems or see them for what they are, facing them head-on?

MEDITATION PRACTICE:

Create more mindful moments throughout your day.

- Set your timer on your phone to go off at set intervals throughout the day (there are also some mindfulness apps that can do this for you).

- When the timer goes off, pause whatever you are doing just for a moment and bring your full awareness to what you see, smell, hear, feel, and taste.

- Don't make up a story in your head about the experience or place any judgment on it. Let it simply be.

- Continue with your day until the next timer goes off again.

- Repeat.

CHAPTER 21

Gratitude

"The attitude of gratitude is the highest yoga."

—*Yogi Bhajan*

Have you ever experienced an overwhelming feeling of gratitude? It's a beautiful experience and something that is hard to put into words.

Maybe you felt it as you stood on the top of a mountain overpass and looked out at the beauty that surrounded you. It's possible you've experienced it as you looked in the eyes of a child and were met with their purity and innocence. Maybe you have experienced it after hearing a family member was in a car accident but walked away unscathed.

Gratitude can be a wonderful feeling and something that we can hold on to when we want to feel good. It can also shift our emotional set point and over time help us become happier and more resilient.

The practice of being grateful and focusing on all the things, big and small, that you can feel gratitude for is getting a lot of attention these days. Research shows that when you shift your perspective and begin to look for all the things you can be grateful for, your life slowly begins to shift as well.

Dr. Henry Emmons, a practicing psychologist and author of *The Chemistry of Joy* and *The Chemistry of Calm,* has spent much of his career researching the effects of a gratitude practice.[26, 27] Dr. Emmons suggests that a gratitude practice can make you happier, and his research supports this claim.

One such study divided participants into two groups. One group kept a weekly journal where they wrote down five things they were grateful for each day, and the other group was asked to write down five things that they were displeased about. The results? After ten weeks, the group who developed a gratitude practice felt better about their lives and were more optimistic about their future. In fact, they were a full 25 percent happier than the other group.

The idea of a gratitude practice isn't new. Oprah has been singing its praises for years and made gratitude journals common by sharing with her readers and viewers how impactful they had been for her. There are books about gratitude and how to incorporate it into your life, apps to help cultivate it, and journals to guide you as you begin your practice.

I will often close my yoga classes by asking the students to find one thing they are feeling grateful for in that moment. Even if life is throwing them a curveball and they feel like things aren't going their way, they can usually find one thing—even if it's simply that they woke up this morning—that they can give thanks for.

Being grateful can shift our entire mindset so that we experience our lives in a new way. We can choose to be miserable, or we can choose to be happy. We can choose to be the victims of our lives, or we can choose to be the heroines.

Life can be incredibly hard, and suffering is prevalent across our lifespan. The first precept in Buddhism is that suffering is universal. But how we respond to that suffering is not. We can be grateful for the simple things in our lives that bring us pleasure, make us smile, and make our hearts happy. Choosing gratitude helps to build our resiliency so that when we are faced with darker times, we can still see the light.

Finding ways to incorporate gratitude throughout your day can be easy. It's about shifting your perspective from time to time and asking yourself what you are grateful for in any given moment. Maybe that's the first moment you wake up in the morning, or maybe it's while you are in the shower or on your drive to work. It could be the moment you hug your kids goodbye on their way to school or greet a friend at work. You don't have to have an entire journal or ritual associated with the practice, although it certainly doesn't hurt. You can simply begin to notice those moments throughout your day when you are thankful for your breath, your ability to move, your community, the people who love you, or whatever else makes your heart happy.

There will be times throughout our lives when we may feel like we are on the top of the world. Cherish those moments for what they are. But we will also experience times that feel like we have plummeted to the bottom of the dark sea. Be kind to yourself during those times, knowing that they can't last forever and, at some point, you will rise back up to the surface. It doesn't mean you don't take the pain with you. It becomes a part of you—sometimes to teach you a lesson, sometimes because it's just the nature of our existence and part of the balance of life.

You always have a choice in how you respond to the ups and downs. You get to choose to accept your emotions and experiences. If you are fully aware of them and allow the energy to move through you, it will eventually lessen. However, if you hold onto the pain and suffering, you give it the power and allow it to fester within you.

Sometimes we can even feel a sense of gratitude for the pain and suffering we experience, as they might open our eyes to a new way or provide us with a beneficial lesson.

Even during the most challenging of times, most of us can find something to feel grateful for. That glimpse of light, however small, might just be the one thing we can cling to that gives us some sense of peace.

JOURNAL EXERCISE:

Take some time to contemplate the following questions and write your reactions to them. Try to allow the responses to flow freely, without overthinking or holding back.

What are the things in your life that you can feel grateful for?

Even if you're in one of the more challenging times in your life, can you still find something that feels a little bit like gratitude?

Do you have a tendency to ignore or stuff your emotions, letting them fester within you?

Can you soften to your more painful emotions, allowing yourself to fully experience them, knowing that it may just help to lessen the suffering?

GRATITUDE EXERCISE:

- Throughout the next week, begin your day by asking yourself what you are grateful for. At the end of each day, reflect on the experiences and moments that you are grateful for.

- When faced with a challenging experience, allow yourself to feel all the emotions. Give them names—anger, sadness, loneliness, etc. Allow the emotion to do its job and move through you (which might take time and coming back to this practice over and over again).

- Finally, find something about the challenging experience that feels a little like gratitude.

CHAPTER 22

Corporate Junkie to Full-Time Yogi

"It does not matter if you are a rose or a lotus or a marigold. What matters is that you are flowering."

—Osho

It has been ten years since I first stepped on my mat during that Friday lunch-hour class. As I reflect on that fleeting moment I experienced in savasana, I realize how far I've come. When I lay on my mat, I was suffering emotionally, physically, and spiritually. My body was responding harshly to stress while my husband was deployed, and I was wondering if there was more to life than what I was experiencing.

I was putting on a mask every morning when I woke up, trying to be tough while falling apart inside. I was slowly moving up the corporate ladder, looking for acceptance while feeling less self-worth and more disconnection.

Yoga wasn't a miracle cure by any means, but when I look at the change and transformation it has created in my life, I'm amazed. I still experience stress, but now I know how to better manage it. I still strive for perfection, but now I recognize it and know how to soften my grip on it. I still have suffering in my life, but I am more resilient and able to handle it.

My circumstances changed with my husband's retirement from the military and our purchase of a yoga studio, but more than anything my acceptance of who I am (perfect, whole, and complete) was the biggest change for me. Yoga has taught me that this outer shell that I lived in wasn't who I was. It taught me that my thoughts and emotions didn't define me. Who I am is greater than all of that. Who I am can't be defined by where I work or what I do.

I am now a fully-fledged yogi. I walk around work barefoot and have learned to actually like green tea. I have donated my business suits and high heels and have vowed to only wear clothes that are comfortable enough to sleep in. Often, the night before I teach a class at six in the morning, I actually do.

I have slowly but surely stepped fully into my new identity. In many ways, I'm still the same person, but I am profoundly changed in other ways. I value a slower pace, I listen to my inner voice with respect and do my best to honor it. I practice a lot more self-care and pay attention when my body sends me messages to slow down or take a break.

I still have that inner voice that tells me I'm not good enough, but the voice isn't quite as loud or frequent. I've learned to cultivate a new voice that helps to counter the old, critical, and self-deprecating part of me. The newer, kinder, gentler voice provides reminders of compassion and self-acceptance when I need to hear it most.

Yoga has changed my life. What I've learned on my mat has filtered out of the yoga studio and has impacted my relationships and my ability to find more happiness and ease in my life, and it has brought my values to the front of my mind. I keep those values close to my chest so that, as I'm making decisions about how to live my life, I'm now choosing to stay in alignment with what is most important to me.

My definition of success has changed. I no longer desire a certain title or specific rung on the ladder. Now, when I hear my friends or family talk about their work aspirations and I hear how much striving they are doing to reach that place where they think they will have "made it," I want to grab them by their shoulders, give them a gentle shake, and tell them there is another way.

But I know better. My path is just that: mine. It's not the right path for most people. It worked for me, and at this moment in my life is still working to teach me the lessons I believe I was destined to learn.

If my story and the mental, emotional, and spiritual transition that has unfolded helps anyone who reads this, I am grateful. Even if it doesn't, I am grateful that my search for enlightenment has led me from corporate junkie to the person I am today.

You don't have to quit your corporate job or make some huge, life-changing decision to experience a glimpse of enlightenment. No matter what your circumstances are, the practices I've outlined throughout this book can help you to achieve contentment, acceptance, and union with self. What I've found along the way is that enlightenment is simply settling into that self, reuniting with it, and knowing that there is another way. You don't have to move through your days with dread, worry, and resentment.

Whether you are ready to make a change or simply want to experience more ease in your daily life, you can use the meditations and guide on the following pages for support. As you begin or continue your own search for enlightenment, know you can find it in the conference room, cubicle, yoga studio, home office, or wherever you are. Just look inside, explore, and find that it is resting quietly in your heart.

PART 3

Enlightenment

CHAPTER 23

Tools for
Mind-Body-Spirit Path

"Yoga allows you to find an inner peace that is not ruffled and riled by the endless stresses and struggles of life."

—B. K. S. Iyengar

You picked up this book for a reason. I'm guessing you might be a corporate junkie yourself and are feeling some of the same feelings of exhaustion and overwhelm that I felt a few short years ago. Maybe you are, or have been, in search of the elusive enlightenment as you feel and know in your heart that there is a better way. Regardless of which category you fit in, I want to leave you with ways that you can explore the practices that have helped me over the years.

Whether you are at the start of your journey or well along the path, the guided meditations on the following pages can be explored from your mat, from your desk, on an airplane, or wherever your life has taken you.

I recommend you try them all and see which ones seem to resonate with you. Which practices leave you feeling lighter and more connected with your inner self? Which ones help you quiet your mind so that you can tame the gremlins and find some peace? Which ones seem most accessible to you and applicable to where you are in your life right now?

It doesn't matter whether you start with three minutes or twenty. What matters is that you are taking some time for you, to practice self-care and to explore what it might feel like to de-stress a bit and calm your body and mind. Over time and with practice, you might begin noticing more ease in your life, a sense of being more connected, and a glimpse of that elusive enlightenment.

Meditations for the Corporate Junkie

BELLY BREATHING:

Sit in a chair or lie on the floor with your hands resting gently on your belly. As you relax in this position, feel your muscles becoming softer and your breath longer. Continue to breathe in and out of your nose, allowing the breath to be soft and steady. Keep your gaze out in front of you or gently close your eyes.

Now start to visualize the breath moving down toward your soft and relaxed belly. As you breathe in, your abdomen will fill with air, and as you breathe out, it will empty. Continue to breathe in this way, feeling the belly fill and press gently against your hands. Visualize the belly filling up from the top to the bottom, from side to side, and from front to back.

Keep breathing in this way, allowing your mind and focus to be on your breathing and nothing else.

When you feel calm and relaxed, feel free to blink your eyes open and take in the sights around you with a fresh perspective.

MINDFUL BREATHING:

You can do this meditation at any time and can be standing, seated, or lying down. You can practice this meditation for a few breaths, several minutes, or longer.

Begin by bringing your awareness to your breath. Notice your inhales and your exhales. As you inhale, silently say to yourself, "I am breathing in." As you exhale, silently say to yourself, "I am breathing out."

Continue for as long as you would like, keeping your attention on your breath.

BODY SCAN:

I would recommend doing this meditation while lying down so that you can completely relax your body. Allow your arms to be resting comfortably at your sides and your legs long.

Relax your body, from the crown of your head all the way down to your heels. Feel your breath become slower and more steady. Draw your focus and attention to the following body parts as you allow yourself to continue to relax deeper, letting go of tension in your body.

- Relax your forehead, eyelids, and jaw.
- Soften your entire face.
- Relax your shoulders.
- Right arm.
- Left arm.
- Feel the beating of your heart in your chest.
- Relax your belly.
- Right hip and buttocks.
- Right thigh, calf, and foot.
- Left hip and buttocks.
- Left thigh, calf, and foot.

Feel your entire body become more and more relaxed as you let all your muscles soften away from your bones. Feel free to continue to lay here as long as you would like or use this meditation to help you relax before falling asleep.

STRESS BUSTER:

This is a great meditation to use when feeling stressed out and needing to get out of fight, flight, or freeze and into your parasympathetic nervous system.

It can be done in a seated position or lying down (although there is a risk you might fall asleep). If you choose to do this seated, sit comfortably with your spine long. Feel your shoulders relax away from your ears and melt down toward the earth.

Bring your awareness to your breathing in and out. Notice the qualities of your breath (long or short, soft or loud, even or uneven). Scan your body from the crown of your head to your hips and notice any tightness in your body. Try to soften and relax those areas of your body.

Now begin to breathe into your lower belly. Feel your belly as you begin to feel the abdomen fill with breath. Notice the gentle rise and fall of the belly as it fills. Continue to breathe into the belly, trying to fill it up completely.

Once you feel as if your breath is filling the belly, with long, steady breaths, begin to draw your breath up towards your heart. Feel the breath fill your abdomen and then rise all the way up toward your chest.

As you exhale, allow the breath to release down toward your belly. Rotate the breath so that the inhales draw your breath up the body and the exhales rotate the breath back down the body.

Continue this breathing, what yogis call pranayama, until you feel relaxed and begin to forget about your stress. Do this practice as often as you need to in order to let go of stress and begin to feel more calm and balanced.

GRATITUDE MEDITATION:

You can do this meditation in conjunction with any of the others or use it as a stand-alone practice.

Begin by focusing on your breath. Take a few big breaths in through the nose and out through the mouth, allowing any stress to release from your body and mind as you exhale.

Breathe in and out through the nostrils and focus on how your breathing feels as it enters and exits your body.

Ask yourself the following question: In this moment, what am I feeling grateful for? Without judgment, notice what comes up for you and feel a sense of gratitude in your heart as you accept your answer.

You can continue to ask yourself that same question over and over again, seeing what comes up for you. When you feel like you've exhausted your answers, you can close out your practice, feeling a sense of gratitude for this powerful exercise.

STOP MEDITATION:

This is a great meditation to practice anytime you notice you are getting worked up or overwhelmed. It is helpful when you notice you are in a reactive mode at work, with your kids, or any other time that you feel as if you aren't in control of your thoughts or emotions.

1. Stop what you are doing

2. Take three deep breaths

3. Observe your body and mind with curiosity

4. Proceed with mindful awareness and intention

Self-Care Tips for the Corporate Junkie

If you are looking for ways to translate a yoga practice into your daily life, this list of six easy things will provide you with things you can do as you move through your days. Some of these may need to be cultivated, as they may not be practices you are used to, but others, like breathing, are things you already do but can bring more focus and intention to.

1. BREATHE

You already take an average of twenty thousand breaths a day. You breathe naturally, whether you are thinking about or noticing it or not. Your breath can provide you with great information about your emotional state. I've even heard people refer to your breath as the "mirror to your emotions" because the qualities of your breath can reflect your emotional state.

The next time you are nervous about a presentation, notice your breath. When you are feeling overwhelmed or anxious, notice your breath. When you are feeling tired or sad, notice your breath. You might begin to notice that, at times, your breath is shallow and jagged and stops in your chest (likely when you are anxious). At other times, your breath might be uneven, with short bursts of breath or long sighs.

The breath that is most beneficial to our physical state is belly breathing. You can find more about this practice in the previous section on meditations for the corporate junkie.

2. MOVE

I remember days where I sat at my desk in my office or cubicle for hours and hours on end without getting up to move. I often ate lunch at my desk (there just wasn't enough time in the day to get all the work done otherwise) and only got up when I absolutely had to—often only to use the restroom.

That kind of sedentary lifestyle will wreak havoc on your body. That's not news to you, I'm sure. You probably already feel the aches and pains associated with sitting. You've likely read that sitting is the new smoking and about how bad it is for our overall health.

There are ways to add more movement throughout your day without having to get to the gym or set your morning alarm an hour earlier. Adding more steps to your day, doing a little chair yoga, or taking the stairs instead of the elevator are simple ways you can add more movement into your days.

One simple practice I used when I was still in the corporate world was to take an extra lap or two around our floor every time I got up the use the bathroom. It only took an extra couple minutes, but it gave my heart a little burst, gave me some renewed energy, and allowed me to clear my mind for a few moments.

3. BE MINDFUL

You've read about the benefits of being more mindful and how your awareness can allow you to notice the beauty in the simple moments throughout your days. Most of us move through our lives missing out on the simple pleasures as we try to check another item off of our to-do list.

Now, I know you still have that list and a million responsibilities. What I am arguing is that without making any major changes to how you spend your time, you can find ways to be fully present in the moment so that you truly experience it.

On a women's retreat, I shared an example from Jon Kabat-Zinn's book, *Wherever You Go, There You Are* about washing the dishes[24]. When you are doing the dishes, allow yourself to just be doing the dishes. Feel the temperature of the water on your hands, the soap on your fingers. Notice the bubbles in the water and the smell of the soap. Be present and allow your awareness of everything else to fade away into the distance.

As you can imagine, a group of ladies on the retreat didn't want to be told they could find pleasure in doing the dishes. However, as we all returned home and implemented these practices, one of the students confided in me that this simple practice changed her perspective and provided appreciation and enjoyment in something she previously considered to be an arduous chore.

4. BUILD COMMUNITY

Think about the people you have spent time with throughout the last week. You might have a busy social calendar and delegated time to be with your community—or, as I like to refer to it, your tribe. However, many of us find very little time throughout our busy days to truly be in community. We may be surrounded by people all day long but still feel alone.

Your tribe is those people around whom you can feel completely yourself. You don't have to pretend to be someone else and you know that they love you just as you are. Maybe that's your family, maybe it's friends, or maybe it's the people at your church, yoga studio, or local pub. It doesn't matter what your community looks like as long as you feel as if you are a part of something and aren't living your life alone.

Don't get me wrong; we all need alone time (some more than others), and I'm not arguing that as an introvert you should force yourself to be an extrovert. But being among like-minded people and being able to talk openly about your fears, your loves, and everything in between is important for our overall health and well-being.

Social media has tricked many of us into believing we have a community of friends, but many of those so-called friends are merely acquaintances we wouldn't even recognize on the street. Our tribes are made of those people who will help to lift us up when we need it most. Be cautious and intentional about how you build your tribe and spend your time.

5. TAKE A BREAK

Do you use your vacation hours? Over my years as a manager, one of my responsibilities was to make sure my staff took their vacation time before the end of the year so that they didn't suddenly request two months off or end up losing the hours they had earned. I can't tell you how surprising it was to me that this was a challenge for people. I had to literally beg people to use their time and remind them that they had earned it and should therefore take the time for themselves.

I also noticed that people often refused to take a day just because they needed some self-care. Instead, they used the time to take kids to doctors' appointments, get work done around their house, or catch up on other responsibilities. Even on vacations, they still had a hard time truly taking a break and taking time off without checking emails.

I always admired the people who planned a day just for themselves and filled it with things that made their heart sing—or at the least brought them back into some semblance of balance. When I worked in social services, we had one day off a year that was not part of our sick leave or vacation leave. It was called a "mental health day." That day was specifically provided for us to use when we were feeling distraught, overwhelmed, and exhausted. We used it when we were at the edge of the cliff and about ready to jump over.

What if you used your time away and took breaks often enough that you didn't reach that edge? What if you took the mental health day or used a vacation day just for you? Maybe you don't have a lot of vacation days to use and are looking for other ways to take a break. How about you put your phone away for an hour or two when you get home at night? What if you stayed away from your email for a weekend so that you could truly unwind and disconnect? Find what works for you, but for the love of all things holy, learn to take a break.

6. FIND GRATITUDE

We've already explored the importance of gratitude a few ways to implement a practice into your daily life. I am going to share a practice here that has helped me deal with the more, ahem, *challenging* people I've met in my life.

We've all had those bosses, employees, or colleagues that drive us crazy. I know, that's not a very yogi thing of me to say, but it's true. We can't inherently like everyone we interact with, since we are all very different beings with different beliefs and values. However, I believe that we can find the good in them and find something that feels like gratitude toward them as individuals.

I learned over the years to not focus on what I believed to be a person's shortcomings or what drove me crazy about them but instead to look for the good in them. What qualities do they bring to your organization or team that are needed? What parts of their personality or perspective are different than others and are therefore filling a needed gap? How can you appreciate what they bring to the table and be grateful for the lessons they bring?

The most challenging of experiences and people will help you grow. If you can't find anything else, at the very least be grateful to them for that.

7. LISTEN TO YOUR BODY, MIND, AND SPIRIT

After accepting my job as a director, I was asked to travel to a conference that would take place during my second full week on the job. Knowing it was necessary to both look like a team player and learn more about the field in which I was working, I agreed and told them to go ahead and book the plane ticket. One of the members of my new team was asked to book the tickets and send me my itinerary.

I remember looking at the flight details in horror when I saw that my colleagues and I were flying out at five in the morning on a Monday. I knew that would mean getting up at three (or earlier) to get to the airport on time. It would also mean that when we arrived and began a full week of sitting through presentations, networking, and meeting other professionals, we would be completely exhausted.

I had learned, from years of work travel and countless trips (but lots of free miles!) to think about the impact the travel would have on my body, my energy, my sleep, and therefore my productivity. I took some direction from Arianna Huffington in her book *Thrive* and realized long ago that it was better to fly out the evening before than to get up before dawn so that I could be well rested and prepared for the day and week ahead. If the company I worked for was willing to spend the money to fly me somewhere, I wanted to put my best self forward.

Needless to say, we were all a wreck the first day of the conference and even into the second day. My mind was foggy, so I drank coffee and consumed sugar to try to stay awake. The cycle began.

How can you make decisions that honor your body, mind, and spirit? Maybe it's respecting your need for a full night of sleep so your body and mind are well rested. It could be that you take the time for a short meditation or breathwork before a big meeting or big day. It might be scheduling that one hour every Friday afternoon over the lunch hour to get to a yoga class. You never know what will happen when you unroll your mat and recommit to finding yourself. I'm so glad I did.

Good luck on your journey to finding a healthier, happier, and enlightened you!

How to Work with Nicole:

I love working face-to-face and virtually with people who want to learn how to implement these strategies into their life for greater health and happiness.

Here are some of the ways that we can work together:

LIFE AND MINDFULNESS COACHING
You picked up this book, so you are likely ready to make a change in your life. As a coach, I can help you uncover what is getting in your way, teach you self-care strategies that work, and provide the accountability to make the change.

INSPIRATIONAL SPEAKER
I love sharing my stories to help inspire others! I would be happy to partner with you or your organization to inspire your audience with humor and authenticity.

BLOGS, WEBINARS, AND COURSES
Visit my website, www.nicolelovald.com, to read my blogs and find out about other webinars and course offerings.

YOGA TEACHER

Teaching yoga has transformed me. I love sharing yoga with others who are looking for a way to de-stress, reconnect with their whole self, and have a little fun. I would love to teach at your festival, conference, or event. Email any inquiries to: nicole@spiritofthelakeyoga.com

Connect with Nicole on Social Media:

 FACEBOOK: facebook.com/nicole.lovald

 INSTAGRAM: instagram.com/nicolelovald40/

References/Citations:

1.   Gina Soleil, "Workplace Stress: The Health Epidemic of the 21st Century," *Huffington Post*, January 7, 2016, https://www.huffingtonpost.com/gina-soleil-/workplace-stress-the-heal_b_8923678.html.

2.   Deborah S. Hartz-Seeley, "Chronic Stress is Linked to the Six Leading Causes of Stress," *Miami Herald*, March 21, 2014, http://www.miamiherald.com/living/article1961770.html.

3.   Brandi Weikle, "4 Ways to Help Your Kids Live Longer," *Today's Parent*, July 8, 2015, https://www.todaysparent.com/kids/kids-health/help-your-kids-live-longer/.

4.   "Stress Index," American Psychological Association, May 2, 2018, http://www.apa.org/news/press/releases/stress/index.aspx.

5.   "Stress Research," American Institute of Stress, May 2, 2018, https://www.stress.org/stress-research/.

6.   Shawn Achor, *The Happiness Advantage* (New York: Random House, 2010).

7. Theo Mertz, "'Nomophobia' Affects Majority of the UK," *The Telegraph*, August 27, 2013, https://www.telegraph.co.uk/technology/news/10267574/Nomophobia-affects-majority-of-UK.html.

8. Glennon Melton Doyle, *Love Warrior* (New York: Flatiron Books, 2016).

9. Alexandra Ma, "A Sad Number of Americans Sleep with Their Smartphone in Their Hand," *Huffington Post*, May 6, 2016, https://www.huffingtonpost.com/2015/06/29/smartphone-behavior-2015_n_7690448.html.

10. "How Stress Affects Your Health," American Psychological Organization, May 2, 2018, http://www.apa.org/helpcenter/stress.aspx.

11. The Center for Mind-Body Medicine Training, Dr. James Gordon, Minneapolis, Minnesota, 2016.

12. Eva M. Selhub, MD and Alan C. Logan, ND. *Your Brain on Nature: The Science of Nature's Influence on Your Health, Happiness, & Vitality* (Hoboken, NJ: Wiley, 2012).

13. Kelly McGonigal, PhD, "Hugging Yourself Reduces Physical Pain," *Psychology Today*, May 21, 2011, https://www.psychologytoday.com/us/blog/the-science-willpower/201105/hugging-yourself-reduces-physical-pain.

14. Gabby Bernstein, *The Universe Has Your Back* (Carlsbad, CA: Hay House Publishing, 2016).

15. Raj Raghunathan, "How Negative Is Your 'Mental Chatter?'," *Psychology Today*, October 10, 2013, https://www.psychologyto-day.com/us/blog/sapient-nature/201310/how-negative-is-your-mental-chatter.

16. Rick Carson, *Taming Your Gremlin* (New York: HarperCollins, 1983).

17. *The Yoga Sutra of Patanjali: A New Translation with Commentary*, trans. Chip Hartran (New York: Shambhala Classics, 2003).

18. Janice Marturano, *Finding the Space to Lead: A Practical Guide for Mindful Leadership* (London: Bloomsbury Press, 2014).

19. Bill George, *Discover Your True North* (Hoboken, NJ: Jossey-Bass, 2015).

20. Jacquelyn Smith, "Here's why workplace stress is costing employers $300 billion a year," *Business Insider*, June 6, 2016, http://www.businessinsider.com/ how-stress-at-work-is-costing-employers-300-billion-a-year-2016-6.

21. Pema Chodron, *When Things Fall Apart: Heart Advice for Difficult Times* (Boulder, CO: Shambhala, 2000).

22. Sheryl Sandberg, *Lean In: Women, Work, and the Will to Lead* (New York: Knopf, 2013).

23. Sheryl Sandberg and Adam Grant, *Option B: Facing Adversity, Building Resiliency, and Finding Joy* (London: W.H. Allen, 2017).

24. Arianna Huffington, *Thrive: The Third Metric to Redefining Success and Creating a Life of Well-Being, Wisdom, and Wonder* (Danvers, MA: Harmony, 2014).

25. Jon Kabat Zinn, *Wherever You Go, There You Are: Mindfulness Meditation in Everyday Life* (New York: Hachette Books, 2005).

26. Dr. Henry Emmons, *The Chemistry of Joy: A Three-Step Program for Overcoming Depression through Western Science and Eastern Wisdom* (New York: Touchstone, 2006).

27. Dr. Henry Emmons, *The Chemistry of Calm: A Powerful Drug-Free Plan to Quiet Fears and Overcome Your Anxiety* (New York: Touchstone, 2010).

Acknowledgments

If you have never had the opportunity to write an acknowledgments page, I encourage you to try it out. It is both a humbling and incredibly rewarding experience to realize all the people in your life that have supported you.

I must start by thanking my husband Jon, who has supported all my crazy endeavors over the years and continues to be my biggest advocate. You are my rock. I am so glad I get to keep living the dream with you.

Thank you to my amazing kids who have both dealt with me saying, "Just give momma one more minute. I need to finish writing this . . ." for over the past two years. Jackson—I learn every day from your kind and compassionate heart. Sofia—your steadfast determination keeps me in constant awe. I love you both with all my heart and am so grateful you call me mom.

I can't thank my tribe of friends enough—thank you all for your continuous support, for keeping me real, and for always laughing at my jokes.

Heidi—I am so happy we were on this journey together and would never have finished this book without our writing retreats. Your humor, support, and love mean the world to me.

My Buddha Belles and Sangha Sisters—We travelled this yoga road together and I am eternally grateful for all that you've taught me over the years.

Mom & Kristen—Thank you for being the first to read this manuscript (when it was in its rawest and likely not-even-readable form). You supported this dream, as you do all my dreams.

To the rest of my family—Thank you for always loving me and being there for me.

Yoga Ted—Your humor and approach to yoga made it accessible to me at a time when I needed it most. Thank you for offering a safe space for me to find myself again.

To the amazing team at Wise Ink—Thank you for not only seeing my dream but providing me with all the tools I needed to make it a reality. Dara B., you are one cool gal. I count myself very lucky to have had the opportunity to work with you.

Finally, to my yoga home and the community that surrounds it. Thank you Spirit of the Lake Yoga and all the teachers past and present. The wisdom you have all shared with me over the years has guided my path and led me to where I am today. I am eternally grateful. Namaste.

About the Author

Nicole Lovald is a former corporate addict turned yoga teacher, life coach, and self-care advocate. She helps people reconnect with their bodies, calm their minds, and live the lives they have imagined for themselves. She is the owner of Spirit of the Lake Yoga and Wellness Center in Excelsior, Minnesota.

Nicole is also a trained counselor who has spent much of her career helping veterans, at-risk children, and victims of violence and abuse. Even during her days of wearing high heels and business suits, she was passionate about helping people overcome adversity, change limiting beliefs, and create a more fulfilling existence.

After fifteen years working in the land of cubicles, she knew something was missing and that she had to listen to her heart's calling and change directions. She found yoga as an avenue for quieting her mind so that she could listen to her intuition to uncover what was missing in her life. She fell in love with how yoga made her feel and slowly learned that it provided her with the answers that she was so desperately searching for.

Going through a teacher training program and learning how to "live her yoga" was the catalyst for major change in her life. She learned how to overcome chronic stress through the self-care practices of yoga, meditation, and breathwork.

Experiencing incredible transformation made her realize how powerful these practices were. She now shares what she has learned through her journey of climbing the corporate ladder to wearing flip-flops and yoga pants.

It is her mission to help others experience similar effects and learn how to step away from the busyness of life and become more present in body, mind, and spirit. A life full of joy, ease, and well-being is her ultimate hope for everyone.